Air War O
Kursk

Turning Point in the East

Dmitriy B. Khazanov

SAM PUBLICATIONS

Air Wars 1
Air War Over Kursk: Turning Point in the East
by Dmitriy Khazanov

First produced in 2010 by SAM Limited, under licence from SAM Publications
Media House, 21 Kingsway, Bedford, MK42 9BJ, United Kingdom

ISBN 978-1-906959-26-5

Typeset – by SAM Publications, Media House, 21 Kingsway, Bedford, MK42 9BJ, United Kingdom
Series Editor – Andy Evans
Translated from the Russian – by Gennady Sloutskiy
Designed – by Simon Sugarhood
Printed and bound in the United Kingdom – by Buxton Press

Contents

Chapter 1

On the eve
of the battle

The 'Grand Battle of Stalingrad' ended in early February 1943 with a total defeat of the German Army, and completely frustrated their plans for a planned summer-autumn campaign of 1942. The German generals considered the rout a disaster – "The defeat in the Battle of Stalingrad terrified both the German people, and the German Armed Forces. Never before had Germany experienced such a terrible loss of so many troops" Westphal wrote. In spring 1943 the Wehrmacht managed to halt the Soviet offensive along the entire front and stabilise the situation, and when developing a war plan for further combat operations along the Eastern Front, the Führer and his generals set far-reaching goals, which also encompassed taking revenge for the defeat in the Battle of Stalingrad, raising the morale of the German Armed Forces as well as the German people, boosting the Reich's prestige with its satellite states, and preventing any break-up of the Axis Powers.

Mistakenly believing that the Red Army had suffered irreplaceable losses in their previous battles, and that it would not be able to restore its strength quickly (taking into account the fact that the Allied Powers were not too eager to open the second front in

❶ Major V.Ya. Gavrilov, HSU, the CO of 81st GvBAP, Voronezh front sector, June 1943 relaxing with P.A. Golovanov (left), and G.I. Gabuniya (right).

⊕ The ceremonial 'Handing the Guards Colours' to the 263rd BAD.

⊕ I.V. Stalin, G.M. Malenkov (VKP/b/ central committee secretary) and N.A. Poskryebyshev (Stalin's secretary) reviewing a captured military equipment exhibition on the eve of the battle for Kursk.

◑ Muscovites view items at the captured military equipment exhibition. Note the Focke-Wulf Fw 200C long-range bomber and the nose section of the Bf 109G fighter at left.

Europe) the German command decided to prepare for a large-scale summer offensive without delay. Lacking sufficient assets for a front-wide offensive, the German command decided to focus most of its strike forces on a narrow part of the front, and deliver a powerful blow against Soviet defences, breach them and then pave the way for an advance into the rear to secure crucial facilities and supply routes. The attention of the German strategists, striving to find the most vulnerable place in the Soviet defence, was attracted to the area around Kursk. The German armies were already in an advantageous position there, as they surrounded the area from the north, the west, and the south. Thus, the German command decided to attack the Soviet troops from all sides. The assumption was that simultaneous attacks from the north-west (outside Orel) and the south-west (outside Belgorod) converging on Kursk, would allow the

↻ The 'Handing of the (challenge) Red Banner' in recognition of the successes in preparing the reserves. The banner is handed by General Belokon (head of the Moscow military District /MVO/political department on the left), to be received by Colonel Lieutenant Kopchaev, the flying school CO.

German forces to envelop and destroy the Soviet armies on the Central and the Voronezh Fronts, and then allow them to mount an all-out offensive. Then, given the successful development of these events, German troops would be able to take Moscow to the rear, and this would have a decisive impact on the outcome of the campaign.

This large-scale offensive would be the cornerstone onto which the German command would pin their far-reaching plans, and this operation was code-named *Zitadelle* (Citadel). This was slated to be the decisive encounter of the Eastern Front in 1943 and would demonstrate the superiority of German military strategy, their greater might and combat capabilities. Hitler also demanded that measures be taken to forestall any Soviet offensive in the Soviet-German Front in the summer.

In order to better manage resources, the German command gave up all previously planned offensive operations as Operation 'Zitadelle' was expected to involve the best troops and the most seasoned commanding officers. The battle planning was personally supervised by Chief of Wehrmacht Army General Staff *Generaloberst* Kurt Zeitzler, while preparations for aviation employment were headed by Chief of *Luftwaffe*, General Staff *Colonel General*

H. Jeschonnek.

In his considerations he stated that:

1. Red Army Air Force units had recently gained extraordinary strength, and their flight personnel were now better trained, had a high morale, and were ready for a large-scale offensive.

2. Since the Soviets were expected to mount a large-scale offensive on the northern side of the Orel-Kursk area, it was necessary to be ready to 'immediately' throw considerable *Luftwaffe* assets into action to counter such an offensive without relaxing efforts outside Kursk.

3. The role of close air support to be provided by the 9th Army to advancing units would considerably increase, given the barely sufficient number of divisions, especially armour divisions, and the lack of artillery.

4. Given the poor supply of advancing troops, which much depended on operation of the Bryansk-Orel railway (which was under constant threat) and a poor road network, the *Luftwaffe* would carry out the function of being the long-range artillery.

5. Transport aviation would play a major role in delivering all necessary supplies for rapidly advancing tank spearheads.

A total of about 1,100 aircraft from the 8th Air

↻ A youngster clambers on a captured aircraft. Note the Dornier Do 17Z in the foreground.

↻ A Bf 109 under repair.

♁ Harmonising the 37mm cannon on a Ju 87G in the firing butts.

Corps were to support the offensive from the south, and about 730 aircraft from the 1st Air Division from the north, and thus most aviation groups were brought up to almost their full strength. Immediately before mounting the offensive, the Germans expanded the network of airfields outside Orel (from three to fifteen) and put all fighters, bombers, and reconnaissance aircraft under the command of the 1st Air Division, with their headquarters in Orel. Only one unit of Squadron JG54 was attached to the headquarters of the 4th Air Division which was established outside Smolensk in June. Thus, although the German command prepared to repulse flank attacks of Soviet air units, the northern part of the front, covered by Army Group Centre, turned out to be considerably exposed. The 4th Air Fleet coordinated its efforts with the 'Army Group South' in the southern flank. During the fierce spring battles in Kuban, most of the 4th Air Fleet units had been attached to the 1st and the 4th Air Corps, and deployed in the Crimea and the Donets Basin respectively. Thus in late June – early July they were redeployed to the northern flank to be assigned to the 8th Air Corps.

It is also worth mentioning the reshuffling in the German 4th Air Fleet. *Generalfeldmarschall* Wolfram von Richthofen, believed to have been the most talented German aviation commander, left for Italy to

♁ The Command of the KG55 *Greif* (bomber wing) at Stalino. From left to right: *Oberstleutnant* O. von Linsingen, *Oberst* E. Kühl (*Geschwaderkommodore*), *Oberstleutnant* W. Quaisner and *Hauptmann* G.K. Höfer. This picture was taken before Operation 'Zitadelle'.

◑ Henschel Hs 126 observation aircraft frequently flew from improvised airstrips.

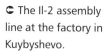

◑ A mobile photographic laboratory belonging to the *Fliegerkorps* VIII HQ.

◖ The Il-2 assembly line at the factory in Kuybyshevo.

➲ *Feldwebel* Navigator G. Leitner from II./KG55 fell into Soviet hands before Operation 'Zitadelle' began.

◑ Induction ceremony into VKP/b/ membership held beside an Il-2 aircraft.

◑ This crew from 99th RAP flew this Pe-2 with M-82 engines – a version produced in only limited quantities.

be succeeded by *General* O. Dessloch, who had previously headed the 1st Flak Corps. Almost at the same time *General* H. Seidemann succeeded *General* Martin Fiebig as Commander of *Fliegerkorps* VIII (the 8th Air Corps). Generals Deßloch and Seidemann, as well as A. Vieirling, Commander of the 25th *Luftwaffe* Administrative Area Command, and R. Reimann, commander of the 1st Flak Corps, were to prepare for the deployment of *Luftwaffe* aircraft during the breakthrough to Kursk from the south. The 4th Air Fleet headquarters sent the following order to the 8th Air Corps in late June: "The main objective is to establish air superiority over the strike force and provide close air support to the 4th Panzer Army and Army Group *Kempf*. Special attention should be paid in focusing efforts over the breakthrough sector of the 2nd SS Panzer Corps. All units, including bomber units, are to engage tactical targets on the battlefield, destroying pillboxes and concentrated artillery. Trains and vehicles should only be attacked if they carry large enemy forces."

It is clear from the distribution of forces that the 4th Air Fleet had exposed its passive flank in the interests of Operation 'Zitadelle' to a greater degree than the 6th Air Fleet, and that elements of the Romanian Air Corps had started to be deployed to the Mius River area in mid-June, as the 1st and the 4th Air

◑ F.F. Arkhipenko from the 27th IAP in the cockpit of his Yak-1 fighter.

➊ On eve of the battle of Kursk, (from left to right) A.F. Moshin HSU, A.Ya. Baklan HSU, I.M. Kholodov, S.F. Dolgushin, the top scoring pilots from 32nd GvIAP, all received the new Yak-9 fighter.

➋ On the eve of the battle, Yak-9T fighters, armed with 37mm cannon, were issued to a number of units of the 16th Air Army, and the 1st GvIAD in particular.

Corps were the only units protecting an area spanning over 600km. The 4th Air Corps operated several air reconnaissance units, light night bomber units, a fighter unit, and an attached Slovak air unit – with a total strength of some 340 aircraft. German documents stated that in the second quarter of 1943 the German aircraft industry had produced just over 2,000 aircraft of various types each month, which allowed the Luftwaffe to beef up its combat and training aviation units on a continual basis. While in late March the Germans operated a total of 6,424 aircraft of various types, by late June this figure had risen to 7,089 and was the first time the *Luftwaffe* had exceeded 7,000 aircraft since the outbreak of WWII. At the same time, the number of aircraft operating in the Eastern Front had been consistently reduced, and on the eve of the Kursk offensive it amounted to less than half of the overall force.

1942 as they had been delivered by 'insignificant forces' and had not followed any sort of plan. The situation deteriorated gradually, but drastic changes took place in spring 1943, when strategic forces started concentrating south of Orel.

The German command was especially concerned about coordinated actions of long-range aviation flight crews and partisan units and arrived at the following conclusion: "Close cooperation between partisans, operating behind the German front line, and enemy front-line units is obvious, and disastrous for delivery of supplies to the army group." German logistic services had a hard time completing preparations for the offensive in late June. For instance, the 1st Air Division had enough munitions (bombs, shells, rounds) for about ten days of a large-scale battle. The situation with fuel was worse; only 5,722 of 8,634 tons of the B-3 aircraft gasoline ordered in June, and

◑ I./JG52 moving to Bessonovka airfield near Belgorod in early June.

◑ Refuelling the Yak-1, note the camouflage netting above.

In late June the German Air Forces in the Eastern Front were weaker than a month before, and this was caused by the adverse air war and the necessity to reinforce air units in Western Europe and Italy. Night-Fighter units were the only air units in the Eastern Front to have been considerably reinforced with five flights, two of which had previously operated as part of the Berlin Air Defence System. Thus, in addition to night-fighter flights from the 4th and the 6th Air Fleets (both units combined operated twenty-six night fighters as of 31 May 1943), Group IV/NJG5, now headquartered in Orel, also joined the battle. On the eve of the battle the Germans had a total of sixty-six night fighters available in the two air fleets, with most of the fighters committed to Operation 'Zitadelle'. Such a considerable reinforcement of night-fighter aviation was caused by the heavy losses inflicted in regular air strikes delivered by the Soviet Long-Range Aviation. According to the Germans themselves, such air strikes had posed no serious threat until autumn

441 of the necessary 1,079 tons of the C-3 high-octane gasoline required by the Fw 190 fighters had been delivered. Hitler and his generals were undoubtedly interested in obtaining the Soviet plans for the 'summer campaign' when preparing Operation 'Zitadelle', and while they had no precise details, they vastly underestimated the combat readiness of the Red Army. This was indicated by the fact that most units were undermanned, and had no idea about operational plans developed by Stalin and the Soviet command, although German documents clearly showed that German headquarters were aware of large Soviet reserves being concentrated outside Kursk. Such data was primarily furnished by air reconnaissance.

The Red Army was initially expected to mount an offensive with the main axis of advance to the south-west in the summer of 1943. The Soviet command based its plans on the fact that it enjoyed an overall superiority over the Wehrmacht as far as available forces and assets were concerned. However, as various

♦ Production of new Messerschmitt fighters in Augsburg.

bits of intelligence on the enemy were obtained, the Supreme High Command General Headquarters and the General Staff were inclined towards going on the offensive, with Marshals A.M. Vasilevskiy and G.K. Zhukov insisting on it. When visiting Kursk the latter sent a report to the Supreme High Command General Headquarters on 8 April, emphasising: "I believe it inexpedient for the Soviet forces to mount an offensive in the next few days in order to forestall the enemy. We had better tire out the enemy, destroy its tanks, throw fresh reserves into action, mount an all-out offensive, and deal a decisive blow to the enemy's major forces." Based on the proposal, Zhukov and

Vasilevskiy developed a draft order for deploying the reserves and establishing the Steppe Front (based on a military district). Stalin approved the order. The decisions taken resulted in concentrating a large group of Soviet troops near Kursk. A 550km part of the front (about 13% of the overall length) saw a concentration of some 28% of servicemen, 24% of guns and mortars, over 33% of combat aircraft, and in excess of 40% of tanks. On the eve of the operation the Red Army enjoyed a 1:4 superiority in personnel, a 1:9 superiority in guns and mortars, a 1:3 superiority in tanks, and an almost 1:6 superiority in aircraft. Table 1 (page 14) gives the strength of some of the Soviet air forces,

★ Table 1: Soviet aircraft deployed at the beginning of July 1943				
Aircraft	**16th Air Army**	**2nd Air Army**	**17th Air Army**	**Total**
Fighters	455/71	389/85	163/43	**1,007/199**
Attack aircraft	241/28	276/23	239/27	**756/78**
Day bombers	260/14	172/23	76/2	**508/34**
Night bombers	74/2	34/15	60/1	**168/18**
Reconnaissance aircraft	4/2	10/8	–	**14/10**
Total	**1,034/117**	**881/149**	**538/73**	**2,453/339**

Note: Figures show serviceable / unserviceable

⌒⌒ Colonel Lieutenant B.N. Vereshchansky, the CO of 614th ShAP issues operational orders to his crews.

꩜ Colonel F.I. Dobysh, the CO of 1st GvBAD, stands with other airmen observing the flight of a Pe-2.

★ **Table 2: Soviet aircraft production in the second quarter of 1943**

Type	April	May	June	Total Period
Fighters	1,164	1,174	1,056	**3,394**
Attack aircraft	1,020	1,005	813	**2,838**
Bombers	372	407	322	**1,101**
Military aircraft total	2,556	2,586	2,191	**7,333**
All types total	3,008	3,031	2,598	**8,637**
Accepted by military acceptance committee	**3,079**	**2,867**	**2,433**	**8,379**

deployed in the main axis of the German advance.

In spring the Soviet Armed Forces were being re-equipped with modern equipment – for instance, the Air Force started receiving an ever increasing number of modified aircraft such as the La-5F fighter, boasting an improved field of view and armour protection; the Yak-9, featuring metal wing spars; the two-seat Il-2 attack aircraft, powered by more reliable AM-38F engines; and the Pe-2 tactical bomber, enjoying better aerodynamics. Aviation units, operating in central parts of the front, had almost no LaGG-3s, Hurricanes, Tomahawks, and Kittyhawks, which had failed to live up to expectations on the Soviet-German Front. The Soviet aircraft industry had made valuable progress in fulfilling the aircraft production programme, shown in Table 2 (page 15).

The organisational structure of forces was improved and streamlined, and strategic reserves were established and beefed up. For example, a total of ten air corps of the Supreme High Command General Headquarters reserve and forty-four manoeuvre air regiments were established in May 1943, and a regiment from each corps started undergoing night training. A total of 3,133 of about 4,000 aircraft sent to the front that month were fielded by tactical aviation units. The same intensity held true for early summer and as a result, some air units were fully equipped (for instance, the 5th Fighter Air Corps, comprising the 294th and the 302nd Fighter Divisions, and the 6th Fighter Air Corps, incorporating the 273rd and the 279th Fighter Divisions), and other units received new aircraft, bringing them up to strength (the 1st Bomber Air Corps received a total of fifty Pe-2s in May alone, and the 1st Attack Aircraft Corps got 58 Il-2s in June). Much attention was paid to flight personnel training, and fighter pilot training improved considerably when flight schools, reserve air regiments, and flight training centres introduced aerobatic training in autumn 1942. Also many of the drawbacks identified in training were rectified in winter-spring 1943, since previous pilots arriving at the front had been ill-prepared for air engagements and had had poor knowledge of German combat techniques and tactics. Such pilots were usually killed in their first combat sorties.

However, all was not running smoothly. The shortage of fuel and the lack of its deliveries to training centres in May considerably hindered pilot training and most aircrew did not manage to log even the mandatory 20–30 hours of flying time. Numerous factory defects, inherent in aircraft and their engines, were reported with the greatest problems being noted

⊙ Major S.P. Tyurikov, the CO of 82nd GvBAP, and a participant in the Kursk air battle.

in the Yak-7bs and Il-2s. Repeated breakdowns of the wing and the fuselage skin caused accidents, and Air Force Commander A.A. Novikov and Air Force Chief Engineer A.K. Repin noted that the blame rested with the aircraft industry, which had reduced its quality control. At the same time factory defects were frequently aggravated by poor workmanship undertaken by ground crews as well as the lack of proper management by senior engineers. In June the Soviet command took urgent measures to rectify this shortcoming and many combat aircraft underwent field repairs, aimed at gluing down plywood skins to wing ribs, restoring paint coats, and rectifying other shortfalls. As a result, the number of unserviceable aircraft was reduced considerably, and most air arms had up to 90% combat-ready aircraft.

Chapter 2
'Zitadelle': The battle begins

As is well known, the German offensive did not come as a surprise to the Soviet side. As part of the main offensive, the German 9th Army command resorted to quite an ingenuous plan of breaching defences on the Central Front. Under this plan a strike force, comprising a spearhead of three Panzer Corps, was to be concentrated just over 40km out. It was then expected to breach the Soviet defences and fight its way through to Kursk along the Orel-Kursk railway and a number of Wehrmacht senior and general officers estimated that Operation 'Zitadelle' would be swift and decisive. The Soviet defence outside Kursk was primarily an anti-tank one. The anti-tank system directly or indirectly comprised every piece of divisional artillery, including rocket-assisted and air-defence artillery guns. The overall concentration of artillery amounted to around thirty-five guns per kilometre on the Central Front, ninety-two guns per kilometre in the 13th Army defence area – which expected to face the main enemy thrust, and up to 125 guns per kilometre at certain other points on the front. In excess of one third of all guns were special anti-tank weapons, however, much attention was also paid to the air defence of ground troops.

A 300km wide area was protected by about 1,000 anti-aircraft guns with two divisions and an independent regiment in place. Most air defence artillery guns were deployed in advance to protect the 48th, the 13th, and the 70th Armies, as well as reinforcements. At the same time air defence regiments and divisions were deployed in tight formations to coordinate their fire. These steps resulted in a high density of anti-aircraft fire at low and medium altitudes. When it became clear that the enemy had completed its final preparations for the offensive, commander of the Central Front General of

↻ An Fw 189A observation aircraft from NAGr15 being camouflaged at the airfield's edge in the Orlov sector.

⋔ Junkers Ju 87D 'Stuka' dive bombers inbound to the target area.

the Army K.K. Rokossovsky ordered a preparatory bombardment, and the artillery from the Central Front started shelling German positions at 02:20 hours. Given insufficient reconnaissance data on enemy defences, most gunners fired their weapons blind, yet still managed to disrupt enemy communications, damage observation posts, and render a great number of guns and mortars inoperative.

At 04:40 hours Moscow time German artillery returned fire at the Soviet troops and the first groups of German aircraft appeared in the sky tasked with breaching the Soviet defences. A total of twenty Ju 88s from II./KG51, flying in an echelon formation at an altitude of about 500m, and at least sixty He 111s from II./KG4, I./KG53, and III./KG53, flying head-on in a 'V' formation at an altitude of 600–2,500m, dropped their deadly payload onto the defensive positions of the 148th Rifle Division, 15th Rifle Corps. Several minutes later three large groups of Junkers bombers from StG1 dived at Soviet artillery positions in the woods and dropped high-explosive bombs, and explosions were also reported to the north of the site. Several air engagements broke out in the small hours of the day and Soviet pilots from the 1st Guards

⋔ Front page of *Volkischer Beobachter* daily from 8 July 1943, and covering the events at Kursk.

Fighter Division managed to shoot down a German dive-bomber. Meanwhile, the air war immediately started developing in an unfavourable way for the Soviet side as the large *Luftwaffe* formations failed to encounter much in the way of resistance from the Soviet fighter patrols. This was possibly due to the fact that units standing at alert on the morning of July 5 were only waiting for an order to engage the advancing enemy! The Germans thus seized the

⋂ An Fw 190 pilot aboard 'Red 9 of III./JG51 is ready for take-off as *Unternehmen Zitadelle* commenced.

⋂ Red Army troops inspecting a shot down Ju 87D dive bomber shot down

⋂ General S.I. Rudenko, the CO of 16th Air Army, seen in discussion with General V.I. Kazakov, the artillery commander of the Central Front sector.

⋂ General of Army K.K. Rokossovsky, the commander of Central Front sector, with his generals and senior officers.

initiative firmly and almost every combat sortie carried out by the *Luftwaffe* was aimed at destroying artillery positions, pockets of resistance, and tanks.

A combined task force, headed by *Major* Kall, received the most powerful air support. His force, which comprised an independent tank battalion equipped with Tigers, and three RGK assault gun battalions, advanced along the railway towards the Ponyri railway station and by 11:00 hours on July 5 VNOS posts (Vozdoushnoe Nablyudenie, Opoveshchenie i Svyaz, or Air Observation, Warning, and Communications) had reported over 1,000 enemy combat sorties, with about 800 of them flown by enemy bombers and dive-bombers.

Never before had *Luftwaffe* acted as long-range artillery to such a degree as it did during the outset of the offensive on the Orel-Kursk area, a fact caused by the lack of sufficient artillery pieces. A total of 3,500 guns and mortars, concentrated by the German 9th

Army on the main axis of advance, faced about 5,000 various artillery systems from the Soviet army. The Soviet Central Front commander ordered the 6th Fighter Corps, comprising the 273rd and the 279th Fighter Air Divisions, to establish air superiority, and these units were the first to go into action and suffer the heaviest losses on July 5. Soviet pilots had to fight uncoordinated air engagements with numerically superior enemy forces, and the strength of Soviet groups was thus reduced considerably after each combat sortie. Those lucky enough to get back to their home bases reported destroying a great number of German aircraft and it would be a safe guess that reports of heavy losses inflicted on the enemy, were expected to slightly relieve the tragedy of the first morning of hostilities.

A group from the 163rd Fighter Regiment sustained heavy losses of five aircraft whilst a group of ten Yak-9s from the neighbouring 347th Fighter Regiment

○ Il-2s head towards their targets.

○ During the battle of Kursk, Junior Lieutenant A.E. Borovykh from the 157th IAP, later twice HSU, was credited with the destruction of six enemy aircraft. Here he stands beside Yak-1 (serial number 1414x), but at the beginning of the battle he flew Yak-1 (serial number 14127).

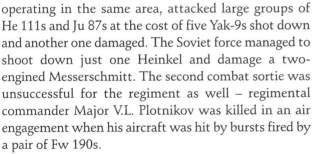

○ The commanding officers of the 92nd IAP from 6th IAK. In July 1943, this regiment was flying the La-5 over the Central Front sector.

operating in the same area, attacked large groups of He 111s and Ju 87s at the cost of five Yak-9s shot down and another one damaged. The Soviet force managed to shoot down just one Heinkel and damage a two-engined Messerschmitt. The second combat sortie was unsuccessful for the regiment as well – regimental commander Major V.L. Plotnikov was killed in an air engagement when his aircraft was hit by bursts fired by a pair of Fw 190s.

German bombers did their best to minimise breaks in the firepower pressure on the Soviet 13th Army. They approached Soviet defensive positions in echelon formations at various altitudes from various directions. The number of enemy bombers was so great that they sometimes had to fly to their targets along the front line, waiting for their turn to deliver an air strike. Soviet fighters could hardly close in with enemy attack aircraft, as they were immediately intercepted by Focke-Wulf patrols. Documents of the 163rd Fighter Regiment

stated: "The number of simultaneous attacks on Soviet positions was so great, that only four aircraft at a time could be sent to fend them off… Each Soviet fighter was countered by six to eight enemy fighters." Air unit headquarters turned out to be unready for such a turn of events and failed to coordinate combat operations in a proper way. Some Soviet air divisions had already been rendered totally ineffective, and reserves had considerably been depleted by 10:00 hours. Ground troops took the fact that Soviet fighters were unable to offer them a reliable protection badly, but were unaware that this was because Focke-Wulf patrols detailed in advance had intercepted Soviet fighters long before they reached the front line.

In most cases the Soviet side failed to bolster its forces due to poor communications and no liaison officers tasked with coordinating Soviet fighters over the battlefield had been allocated in advance. The battle then saw its first critical moment as the large

🎧 A Douglas Boston bomber from the 221st BAD at an operational airstrip west of Kursk.

🎧 A repair team working on a U-2 from 271st NBAD in the Central Front sector, 6 July.

🎧 On 5 July 1943, *Oberfeldwebel* G. Strassel from III./JG51 was credited with the destruction of fifteen Soviet aircraft.

German tank spearheads charged towards the villages of Ponyri, Snova and Podolyan. The Central Front command ordered the commanding officer of the 2nd Panzer Army to redeploy his units to the breakthrough area and also threw all available tactical reserves into action. The aircraft which had been standing at alert were ordered to scramble two bomber divisions to seal off the breach in the 13th Army defences, and concentrate up to 200 fighters in areas of particularly active German operations.

The battle plan from the outset envisioned a third of all attack aircraft flying combat missions at the request of front-line units, while the rest, joining with all available bombers, were to remain in the reserve to be employed in massive attacks against penetrating enemy units. The 16th Air Army had decided to throw attack aircraft into action by midday and aircraft from the 241st and the 221st Bomber Divisions were the first to attack German tanks and infantry. The overall number of aircraft involved were around about 150 Pe-2s and Bostons and by early afternoon they began

delivering air strikes against the enemy forces. Since the *Luftwaffe* offered fierce resistance in the air, several fighter regiments from the 279th Fighter Division were also allocated to protect the bombers. Sorties flown by Soviet bombers, especially Pe-2s, which delivered bomb strikes in a shallow dive, turned out to be very successful. The German infantry was cut off from its tanks, which did not want to risk advancing under heavy artillery fire, and took cover.

The attack aircraft squadrons suffered from poor teamwork and mutual fire support within their units and these factors became a primary cause of heavy losses in aerial engagements. The 299th Attack Aircraft Division, manned with quite a few young pilots, suffered the heaviest losses but the 2nd Guards Attack Aircraft Division, which operated as part of the 16th Air Army as well, was more successful due to the considerable combat experience of many of their flight crews, gained during the Battle of Stalingrad. On July 5 pilots from the 2nd Guards Attack Aircraft Division used new PTAB-2.5-1.5 shaped-charge bombs for the first time and reported killing thirty-one German tanks that day, losing three Il-2s in the process. Another Il-2 had to be written off due combat damage and these attack aircraft were protected by fighter units of the 283rd and the 286th Fighter Divisions. When escorting bombers, the 279th Fighter Division, the 6th Fighter Corps, didn't suffer any considerable losses, while follow-up patrol missions proved to be really devastating. Divisional units, equipped with an average of twenty-four combat-ready La-5s, operated in groups of sixteen to eighteen aircraft aircraft. Despite their considerable strength, they were not able to frustrate many enemy bomb strikes, but lost great number of aircraft and pilots – for instance, a total of six fighters did not return from a combat sortie, which was flown by a group from the 486th Fighter Regiment, headed by Major D.A. Pilipets.

A group of 18 La-5s, tasked with protecting friendly ground troops outside Ponyri, was flying in an air stack formation at an altitude of 3,000 to 4,000m and when the strike force charged at a group of nine Ju 88s, the upper team of four La-5s were already pursuing a pair of Focke-Wulfs above the cloud cover and did not take part in the ensuing air engagement. The strike force dispersed after the first attack, and one of the leaders, Captain Ovsienko, carried out a sharp combat turn, but his less seasoned wingmen were not able to follow suit and dropped behind. On noticing Ju 88s, a group of four aircraft, led by Major Pilipets, attacked as well, but when recovering, the commander's aircraft was hit. Major Pilipets bailed out over the enemy territory and never made it back. The Soviet pilots managed to hit just one Fw 190 in the dogfight.

The results of the first day of air engagements over the Central Front were as follows: *Luftwaffe* fighter aviation played a major part in establishing air superiority. Pilots from Squadron *Mölders* started patrolling the forward edge of the battle area and its southern approaches, intercepting groups of Soviet aircraft in the early morning of 5 July. Unbiased enemy documents state that on 5 July a total of 522 Focke-Wulf combat sorties were countered by 817 Soviet fighter missions. Even if about sixty sorties, flown by Messerschmitt reconnaissance aircraft from NAGr4, which took an active part in air engagements over the 41st Tank Corps, are taken into consideration, the ratio of fighters, involved in air engagements, was clearly not in favour of the Germans. The average number of

↻ With 132 sorties completed since the onset of the conflict, Captain P.P. Pospyelov (pilot) and Senior Sergeant V.M. Vlasov, with fifty-eight sorties, were one of the most experienced crews of the 58th GvShAP in the Orel-Kursk sector.

combat missions flown by a serviceable German fighter that day amounted to three and a half sorties, while an average Soviet fighter flew just over two missions.

Soviet pilots also gave the initiative to the enemy since they could pick the time and the place for their attacks and the majority of the seventy-six air engagements fought on July 5 started unfavourably for the Soviet pilots. *Luftwaffe* aces claimed most of the day's 166 air victories, with over fifty of these being reported by Group III./JG51 and pilot H. Strassl of III./JG51 scored a truly amazing number of fifteen air victories. Later on the Germans revised the results of that day, stating that "a total of exactly 120 Bolshevik aircraft were destroyed." It should be noted that German ground observers were quite precise in counting the number of Soviet aircraft shot down, since the 16th Air Army headquarters reported losing ninety-eight aircraft.

Official German sources state that such outstanding results were achieved at the expense of only seven aircraft lost. However, the list of losses suffered by groups and squadrons of the 1st Air Division on 5 July 1943 gives a different figure: thirteen aircraft were shot down behind the front line, and thirty-three more sustained heavy damage, with twenty-two of them having to be written off later on.

Given the fierce resistance, offered by the Soviet anti-aircraft artillery, the ratio of irreplaceable losses suffered in air engagements can be assessed as 4:5.

Fighters accounted for most of the losses of the 16th Air Army. For instance, the 6th Fighter Corps lost forty-five aircraft. These heavy losses affected the operation of Soviet attack aviation – as, given the lack of sufficient escorts, the number of combat sorties per each serviceable attack aircraft amounted to less than one on the first day of the battle, while day bombers featured a ratio of one combat sortie per two serviceable aircraft. Each combat-ready He 111 or Ju 88 in service with the German 1st Air Division conducted three to four sorties, and each Ju 87 carried out at least four to five sorties. The overall weight of German bombs, dropped on Soviet troops, equalled about 1,500 tons, which exceeded the number dropped by the Soviet aviation almost twelve-fold.

When evaluating the initial results of the battle the German command considered it necessary to appreciate the *Luftwaffe's* exceptional role in the initial success of the offensive. "Successive waves of large aviation forces provided an excellent support to the ground offensive. Numerous direct hits against enemy artillery batteries, field positions, and transport convoys were reported. They resulted in killing three enemy batteries, three

⋔ Newsreel cameraman I. Sholokhovich visits one of the La-5 units of the 16th VA.

◑ German troops inspecting a shot-down La-5 fighter.

◑ German troops hiding from a Soviet air attack take cover beneath a destroyed T-34 tank.

◑ A flak unit from the 12th motorised division in action.

tanks, and a great number of motorcars, as well as rendering several batteries inefficient. The fighter aviation, tasked with conducting escorts and repulsing enemy air strikes, achieved great success". However, it is worth mentioning that the Soviet defence was quite ready for enemy air strikes. Pillboxes, a network of trenches, and well camouflaged positions minimised losses suffered through enemy air strikes and guns; those inside pillboxes could only be rendered out of action by a direct bomb hit. Multiple back-up wire communication lines had been laid in advance, as well as a wide employment of radio stations, allowing the 13th Army headquarters to exercise reliable command and control over every reinforcement unit.

Certain tank regiments and self-propelled artillery units, constituting army reserves, suffered almost no losses that day. The fact that the *Luftwaffe* concentrated its efforts primarily on the forward edge of the battle area allowed the second echelon of the Central Front, including the 2nd Tank Army, two independent tank corps, and a rifle corps, to start redeploying without loss on the night of July 5. German documents also pointed out a successful operation by the 12th Air Defence Division. According to a report of the 6th Air Fleet, anti-aircraft gunners suppressed 66 weapon emplacements, destroyed an air-defence battery and a Katyusha multiple-launch rocket system in the course of the ground battle. Stalin, who remembered the impact of German aviation on the outcome of ground battles in 1941–1942, interrupted Rokossovsky's evening report with the following question: "Did you manage to establish air superiority?" On getting an evasive response, Stalin was not satisfied and asked Rokossovskiy another question: "Will Rudenko be able to cope with the task?" The Supreme Commander-in-Chief was repeatedly informed that the Soviet Air Force at least was not inferior to the enemy as far as its strength and materiel quality were concerned but the future marshal was in for trouble. Then, Rokossovskiy decided to personally shoulder the burden of responsibility and promised to establish air superiority as early as the following day. Unfortunately, this most famous of famous Soviet military leaders was unable to deliver on his promise.

The battle came back with a vengeance as on the morning of 6 July about twenty-five Bostons from the 221st Bomber Division, escorted by about the same number of Yak fighters from the 282nd Fighter Division, delivered the first of four strikes against the German 47th and 41st Corps. They were only countered by small patrols of Messerschmitt reconnaissance aircraft, which could not disrupt the Soviet attack. Pilots from the 221st Bomber Division and the 282nd Fighter Division carried out several run-ins on enemy targets, and attack aircraft from the 2nd Guards Attack Aircraft Division and the 299th Attack Aircraft Division, escorted by fighters from the 283rd and the 286th IAD (Istrebitelnaya Aviatsionnaya Diviziya, or the Fighter Air Division), operated in similarly large groups.

The very first air strikes against the enemy proved that Soviet aviation had poor liaison with its own ground troops on the battlefield and an aviation liaison officer from the command and control post of the 13th

Army managed to scramble aircraft to the battlefield quickly and even tried to coordinate their efforts, but air strikes still failed to coincide with the offensive, mounted by the 17th Guards Rifle Corps, in either time or place. Bomb strikes failed to hit enemy defensive areas on the main axis of the Soviet advance, and in a number of cases such bomb strikes managed to hit friendly troops. This was partially caused by the rapidly changing situation on the ground and the inability of the aviation liaison officer at the army command and control post to update air units on the battlefield environment. Air engagements fought on 6 July were even more violent than those on the day before, and Soviet documents reported a total of ninety-two air battles. According to the Red Army command, German fighter aviation, which had primarily escorted its bombers the day before, changed its tactics on 6 July. The Germans now detailed powerful fighter groups to clear the airspace of Soviet patrols.

Air engagements were long and intensive, although, as a rule, Soviet pilots had to engage enemy fighters, rather than bomber or dive-bomber groups. For instance, a group of seventeen La-5s from the 92nd IAP, tasked with patrolling the sky over friendly ground troops, detected and attacked up to forty Ju 88s. As the La-5s dispersed in the dense cloud cover, Focke-Wulfs arrived and contained the Soviet pilots, who tried to repulse enemy attacks in pairs and independently, but

↻ A Yak-1 at an operational airfield.

⋂ Senior Lieutenant I.V. Kuznetsov from the 30th GvIAP seen here in an Airacobra recalls his recent sortie. Kuznetsov was credited with eleven victories, both solo and shared.

their efforts were uncoordinated. As a result, a total of eight pilots, including a squadron leader, Hero of the Soviet Union, Captain I.D. Sidorov, did not return to their home base. That particular dogfight was typical in many respects and similar to air engagements of the previous day when fighters of the 16th Air Army failed to disrupt enemy bomb strikes once again.

Luftwaffe forces were especially active in the Olkhovka direction, defended by the 17th Guards Rifle Corps, the 13th Army. According to the report of the front commander, "the enemy aviation, operating in groups of twenty to thirty and 60–100 aircraft, delivered non-stop air strikes against Soviet combat formations there." Many other Soviet units came under enemy air attacks as well. Figures in German reports state that the intensity of combat missions flown by the 6th Air Fleet was reduced more than two-fold on the second day of the battle. Such a reduction was primarily caused by the huge strain of the previous day's fighting. In addition to that, the number of serviceable German aircraft decreased due to losses and damage suffered and had an impact on the overall combat readiness of German units as well. All these

factors made the German command concentrate its efforts on narrow parts of the front; even to a greater extent giving an impression of non-stop mass air strikes on Soviet ground troops. According to German situation reports, fighters from the 1st Air Division were extremely efficient on 6 July when they scored 118 air victories in 317 combat sorties. Pilots from III./JG51 achieved the best results among German aviators and H. Strassl kept increasing his astonishing record by shooting down ten more Soviet aircraft that day! Fighters accounted for most of the Soviet aircraft losses (a total of ninety-one aircraft) with the 6th Fighter Corps suffering the greatest losses – a total of eighty-one aircraft and fifty-eight pilots from the outset of the battle, and now had only forty-eight combat-ready fighters left by the following morning.

Although the 1st Guards IAD suffered fewer irreplaceable losses, the number of combat-ready aircraft in the division equalled only twenty-six Yak-1s and Yak-9s (excluding aircraft in the inventory of the 67th Guards IAP, which still remained in the reserve). S.I. Rudenko reasonably feared that several more days of combat operations would push the fighters of the

16th Air Army to the brink of a disaster. He appealed to Zhukov to ask Stalin for permission to redeploy the 234th IAD from the 15th Air Army to the Central Front. However, the efficiency of German pilots should not be overestimated. Numerous reports of German aviators destroying Soviet armoured targets should be considered with care. For instance, on 6 July they claimed to have totally destroyed twenty-nine tanks and damaged twelve more vehicles.

The German command admitted that it had managed to repulse counterattacks, launched by Soviet tanks and infantry by throwing the considerable reserves of the 9th Army into action rather than delivering bomb strikes. The Soviet 2nd Tank Army became the primary target for the attacks of German bombers and dive-bombers on that day and the following few days, and reports from the German 1st Air Division stated that a total of seventy-four Soviet tanks had been destroyed by 11 July. In fact, the 2nd Tank Army lost a total of 214 tanks within that period of time, with 138 of them being irreplaceable losses and only nine tanks destroyed as a result of enemy air strikes, and this was partially caused by the powerful Soviet air defence system.

On the second day of the battle the Soviet command redeployed two small air defence artillery regiments and a medium air defence artillery regiment, previously tasked with protecting facilities in the rear, into the defensive area of the 13th Army, and moved other units to an area outside Ponyri to build-up forces in the most critical directions. As early as 6 July, most senior and general officers of the German 9th Army realised that advancing German forces had been dragged into fierce combat by well-equipped Soviet defensive positions. Despite the commitment to combat of two tank divisions from the second echelon and *Luftwaffe's* massive support, the 47th Panzer Corps had not been able to counter surprise attacks of Soviet tanks by the turn of the day. Divisions from the 46th and the 41st Panzer Corps, advancing on the flanks, crept their way forward at an extremely slow pace; however, constant redeployment of fresh Soviet reinforcements from the rear stopped them crushing the resistance of the Red Army.

German commanders reported to the *Führer* that German soldiers fought heroically, German aviation had operated beyond praise, destroying 642 Bolshevik aircraft at the expense of insignificant losses, but the enemy had been aware of the plans and the time of the German offensive, and no element of surprise had been achieved. The battle on the ground and in the air continued round-the-clock.

Soviet command adjusts aviation activities

The Soviet command had committed considerable reserves to combat and was eager to get reports about drastic changes with regards to air superiority. When a considerably smaller number of German aircraft

◑ Exposed film is removed from the Pe-2 reconnaissance aircraft from the Central front sector.

Ω A crew stands beside the nose section of a Douglas Boston bomber from the 221st BAP.

appeared over the battlefield on 7 July, this was taken as a positive sign. It was not by chance that on the third day of hostilities Red Army Air Force Commander Marshal A.A. Novikov sent a directive "On eliminating drawback in operations of the Air Force" to commanding officers of air armies and air corps. Here Novikov stated that senior commanding officers did not assess their capabilities properly, did not take enemy resistance into account when assigning combat missions, and did not bear responsibility for combat missions, the main objective of which was "to make a sortie, rather than discharge the task". He also pointed out the lack of initiative and warcraft among flight crews with insufficient reconnaissance of enemy targets prior to delivering an air strike, poor cooperation among various aviation combat arms, a passive employment of the fighter aviation and its poor radio guidance, as well as stereotyped employment and the poor defensive capabilities of attack aircraft.

The Red Army Air Force command managed to reduce its losses per combat sortie by introducing order and discipline in the air and on the ground, and a total of just eighty-seven aircraft were written off on 7 and 8 July. Thus, aircraft losses almost halved compared

with those suffered during the first two days. This also resulted from a decrease in German fighter aviation activities, as many Focke-Wulfs had been put out of action and on July 8 it became clear that even the best *Luftwaffe* fighter pilots were not immune to bad luck!

Following a swift attack from a high altitude, which resulted in the shooting down of a Yak fighter, Oberfeldwebel H. Strassl of III./JG51 started recovering his Fw 190 from a dive to a steep climb. When the aircraft levelled out at an altitude of about 4,000m, its speed dropped and it took the heavy fighter several agonising seconds to accelerate, and as luck would have it Soviet fighters were patrolling the sky at various altitudes, and one of the units from the 347th IAP immediately went after the German aircraft. On seeing the danger, Strassl plunged his aircraft into a dive again and descended 3,000m, but the leading Yak-9 kept up. On closing to a range of 80m, Captain Silukov fired several accurate cannon and machine-gun bursts and saw the enemy fighter blaze and crash into the ground just outside the village of Khitrovo. Strassl, who had scored a total of sixty-seven victories in 221 combat sorties, tried to bail out, but his parachute did not release at a low altitude and he was killed.

Many historians believe that 7 July became the breaking point in the ground battle at the northern sector of the Orel-Kursk area. Soviet attack aviation made a considerable contribution to this end as attack aircraft flew 219 combat sorties on that day. Bomb strikes against the German 9th Panzer Division, headed by *General* Scheller and deployed outside Kashary (the Olkhovka direction), involving anti-tank bombs turned out to be particularly efficient. These strikes were conducted by groups of thirty to forty Il-2s from the 299th Attack Aircraft Division, protected by powerful fighter escorts, and pilots claimed to have destroyed at least thirty-four enemy tanks and armoured vehicles. A wide use of shaped-charge bombs also yielded positive results, since concentrated forces of enemy tanks, assault guns, and armoured personnel carriers proved to be extremely vulnerable to air strikes. Groups of eight aircraft, led by Senior Lieutenant Smirnov and Captain Strashnov from the 874th Attack Aircraft Regiment, carried out numerous combat missions, and on returning from one such sortie the two leaders were commended by the 13th Army Command.

On that day the Soviet command committed all three bomber divisions of the 16th Air Army to combat, with the 241st Bomber Division going into action as well. Reports recorded a total of 235 bomber sorties, which was twice as many as on the two previous days combined. Bomb strikes, delivered by Soviet Petlyakov bombers and Bostons, came as a total surprise for the German command. Pilots from the 299th Attack Aircraft Division faced the toughest challenge. When delivering an air strike against enemy ground troops in the afternoon, a group of 11 Il-2s came under a head-on attack, which was a rare event, but the Soviet pilots managed to avoid any losses. However, Focke-Wulfs managed to distract the Soviet escort fighters and attacked the Il-2s again. So the Soviet pilots had to descend to 15–20m and repulse some thirty attacks.

Other divisional units turned out to be less lucky. July 9 proved to be one of the most unfortunate days in the history of the division as their headquarters constantly received reports of attack aircraft downed and crews killed or missing in action. While on the morning of July 5 the division had 142 flight crews and 142 combat-ready attack aircraft, four days later its strength had more than halved. On 9 July the German 1st Air Division carried out 877 combat sorties, while the Soviet 16th Air Army made 775 sorties. The Luftwaffe had enjoyed air superiority since the outset of the German offensive, dropping more bombs and carrying out more combat sorties a day (save for 6 July) than Soviet aviation, and clashes sometimes operated with the same intensity at night as during the day. German air defence gunners and searchlight operators from the 12th Air Defence Division were the major enemy for Soviet pilots at night.

◊ In summer 1943, the Pe-2 was the mainstay of the VVS bomber arm.

⟲ Pilots of *Staffel* 1 from JG51 seen between sorties.

↻ *Generalfeldmarschall* von Kluge – the Commander of the *Herresgruppe Mitte*.

↻ *Gruppekommandeur Hauptmann* F. Losigkeit, of III./JG51 is satisfied with his sortie!

At the first stage of the battle German night fighters did not patrol the front line. That was the probable reason for insignificant losses of the Soviet 271st Night Bomber Division; a maximum of four to five aircraft were damaged. German *Störkampf* 'night-harassing units' from the 6th Air Fleet suffered the same losses of four to five aircraft within the first five days of hostilities. At the same time two other attack aircraft and their pilots were captured by the Soviets, and an Ar 66 crashed several kilometres away from the Orel-Severnyi airfield, killing the crew. While being unable to accurately assess losses inflicted on the enemy within the first five days of the battle, and almost always exaggerating them, both sides could certainly evaluate their own losses. There is no doubt that the Red Army Air Force had sustained far greater damage than the Luftwaffe did, but nevertheless Soviet units remained combat ready. Table 3 gives an idea of changes in the strength of the 16th Air Army.

When changes in strength are evaluated, it is worth taking into account that the Soviet air forces were reinforced with about 200 aircraft, including 107 fighters (with sixty-seven of them in a combat-ready condition) delivered to three regiments of the 234th Fighter Division, deployed at the Central Front. Irreplaceable losses, suffered on 5–9 July, amounted to 330–340 aircraft, including a number of long-range bombers, while some heavily damaged aircraft were submitted to undergo repairs. The 6th Air Fleet scrapped about eighty to ninety aircraft within that time, with fighters accounting for about half of the aircraft scrapped. It is a certain fact that Squadron JG51 Mölders had lost some thirty-seven Fw 190s of various marques by the morning of 10 July, and an even greater number of fighters were damaged and temporarily put out of action. Thus, the German command decided to reinforce fighter aviation operating on the northern sector of the Orel-Kursk area, with a new aviation group. Group II./JG54, which had previously operated outside Leningrad, was also ordered to redeploy to an area outside Orel. As of the morning of 10 July the strength of the German air forces was approximately 650 aircraft (excluding air transports, liaison planes, and other auxiliary aircraft). Thus there were no significant

★ Table 3: Change in strength of 16th Air Army between 5 and 10 July 1943				
Aircraft type/date	As of 5 July 1943		As of 10 July 1943	
	Aircraft total	Serviceable	Aircraft total	Serviceable
Fighters	526	455	440	311
Attack aircraft	269	241	168	119
Day bombers	274	260	251	197
Night bombers	76	74	75	71
Reconnaissance planes	6	4	11	8
Total	1,151	1,034	954	706

changes in the balance of forces.

After holding a meeting with Commander of the 9th Army *Generaloberst* W. Model, *Generalfeldmarschall* Gunther von Kluge decided to revise the nature of combat operations on 10 July. He reported to the *Führer*: "The advancing troops managed to move forward by only two to three kilometres due to fierce enemy resistance. Since no quick success has been achieved, we now face the objective of inflicting maximum losses on the enemy at the cost of minimal own losses. We have started bringing up the reserves with this end in view". Hitler believed it too premature to give up the idea of encircling and destroying the Soviets in the Orel-Kursk area so Von Kluge was ordered to play for time and hold the advantageous position. He was to do his best not to give the enemy any breaks and as soon as von Manstein had achieved operational success, around one third of the attack aircraft in service with the 4th Air Fleet would be handed over to the 6th Air Fleet to finally crush the Soviet defences. The battle on the ground and in the air continued on July 10 and just as on previous days, attack aircraft from the 16th Air Army kept delivering powerful air strikes against enemy forces, reserves, artillery positions, and tanks. Flight crews from the 221st Bomber Division operated with considerably more success than before, however; according to documents available the major burden of combat missions was shouldered by the 3rd Bomber Corps.

German flight crews also delivered intensive bomb strikes against Soviet defensive positions and whilst Soviet attack aircraft made 252 combat sorties during the day, German bombers and dive-bombers conducted 595. In addition, German twin-engined fighters carried underwing bombs on over fifty sorties. The ratio of overall number of combat mission undertaken on 10

July was 671 Soviet against 1,136 German (and 921 versus 1,227, if night sorties are taken into account). However, the worst thing was that Junkers and Heinkels were now operating with the same impunity as on the first few days of hostilities. Numerous reproaches were thrown at the pilots from the 16th Air Army and many commanding officers admitted that such actions were quite were justified. For instance, Commander of the 279th Division Colonel F.N. Dementiev noted to his regret: "All our fighters carry out patrols about ten kilometres to the rear of the front line unwilling to approach the forward edge of the battle area for fear of enemy anti-aircraft fire, and thus they enable enemy bombers to wheel over their targets for hours." His conclusion is extremely bitter: "I am ashamed for them."

The reaction of the German command to Soviet air strikes is unknown but there is no doubt that cars, carrying infantry, armoured personnel carriers, and tanks turned out to be very vulnerable to the massive employment of small anti-tank bombs. The 6th Air Fleet command must have realised that even given the intensive employment, the number of combat-ready Focke-Wulfs was clearly insufficient and in addition to that, only one unit of the promised Group II./JG54 arrived at the front to reinforce the 1st Air Division on 10 July, and another one arrived a day later, while 4./JG54 stayed behind at the Krasnogvardeysk airfield outside Leningrad throughout the Battle of Kursk. Captured German documents said that German commanding officers constantly demanded that losses be replenished, but their requests were only partially met, and then with great delays.

Meanwhile, the drive of German ground troops slackened considerably, since they had almost ran out

U An Fw 190 after a forced landing into Soviet-held territory near Ponyri village.

⟨⟩ A Soviet AA range-finder operator in action.

of fresh reserves, and on 11 July the enemy halted its offensive altogether, withdrawing its tank divisions to the rear awaiting reinforcements. Given this fact and the losses suffered, Soviet aviation drastically curbed its activities and bad weather made a contribution as well. The Germans suffered their heaviest loss on 11 July, when the commanding officer of IV./JG51 *Major* Rudolf Resch (ninety-three air victories) was killed in action. Soviet pilots prevented the commander of IV./JG51 from reaching the magic number of 100 air victories. Although certain German reports state that Resch fell victim to anti-aircraft artillery fire, Soviet sources, as well as interrogation of German POW's, prove that Major Resch was shot down by pilots from the 234th Fighter Division over Maloarkhangelsk. He must have been shot down by Senior Sergeant Kirov – as the young pilot hit the cabin and the fuselage of Resch's Focke-Wulf at point-blank range. As is known, the battle entered a new stage on 12 July, when the Bryansk Front mounted an offensive. German units had started redeploying to go on the defensive even a day or two before that and it became obvious that both the Commander of Army Group Centre *Generalfeldmarschall* Gunther von Kluge, and Commander of the 9th Army *Generaloberst* W. Model, finally gave up their plans to fight their way through to Kursk from the north.

On recovering from the initial shock caused by an unusually massive deployment of aviation by the enemy, Soviet pilots soon started offering an active resistance, and according to documents a total of 7,548 combat sorties were carried out on 5–12 July, with 1,400 of them made at night. As early as the second day of

⟨⟩ A destroyed APC with an anti-tank cannon.

the battle Soviet pilots started operating in large groups to counter advancing enemy units, and seeking out the tank units. The main objective of frustrating the enemy offensive, set by the Soviet command, was fulfilled by and large, although Soviet pilots failed to provide their own ground troops with reliable protection. Within the first eight days of hostilities the 16th Air Army lost 391 aircraft as the Soviet command spared no effort to establish air superiority, and a total of 62% of all daytime sorties were carried out by fighters (1,800 combat sorties were aimed at providing close air support, and 2,057 sorties at escorting attack aircraft and bombers).

However, the aim of establishing air superiority had not been realised by the end of the defensive battle and passive resistance was the primary cause of Soviet failures. Soviet aviation did not make a single daytime air strike against enemy airfields, or attempt to destroy enemy aircraft on the ground, or contain enemy fighters on the approaches to the front line. Although passive

⋂ A Junkers Ju 87D from StG2, shot down south of Orel.

⋂ Loading bombs – ten FAB-100 munitions, seen here on the ground, were the standard Il-4 warload.

combat operations undertaken by the Soviet fighters reduced the efficiency of the fight for air superiority, they were not the only reason that prevented the Soviet side from capitalising on its numerical superiority. Soviet pilots operated with far less intensity than German flight crews and in addition to that, poor command and control had a major impact.

Before the outset of the battle the 6th Air Fleet command had ordered its fighter pilots to prevent Soviet aircraft from reaching the front line, thus providing their own attack aircraft and ground troops with 'freedom of action'. In the course of the battle the German command arrived at the conclusion that the best way to defend their own forces was to destroy as many enemy aircraft as possible, which would also serve to exhaust the Red Army Air Force. German aces made much progress at that and played a decisive role in securing the ratio of losses in their favour. It was only on rare occasions that they returned home without rocking their wings, meaning they had scored another air victory. Although reports of the 6th Air Fleet stated that within the first week of Operation 'Zitadelle' a total of 596 Soviet aircraft were shot down, sixty-five aircraft were destroyed by the 12th Air Defence Division, and about 100 aircraft were hit by air defence fire, it is clear from the facts mentioned above, that Soviet documents confirm just about half of German victory claims.

Lavochkin La-5 'White 65', 302rd IAD, Skorodnoye airfield, July 1943

The aircraft is painted in the colours standard for this fighter type in the first half of the war: AMT-4 green with AMT-6 black blotches on upper surfaces, and AMT-7 light blue on lower surfaces. Note the light blue fin cap. Red stars have black trim.

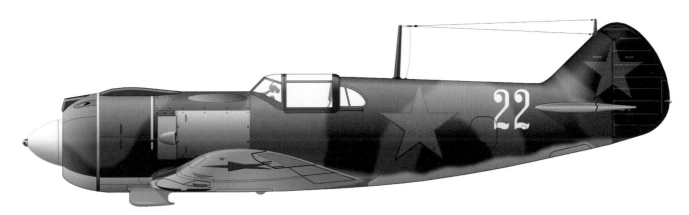

Lavochkin La-5 'White 22', 279th IAD

This aircraft was hit by German fighters in the vicinity of Orel and force landed in enemy territory. The aircraft is painted in the colours standard for this fighter type in the first half of the war: AMT-4 green with AMT-6 black blotches on upper surfaces, and AMT-7 light blue on lower surfaces. Note the White spinner. Red stars have black trim.

Lavochkin La-5 'White 04', 88th Guards IAP

On the eve of the Kursk battle, Junior Lieutenant A.V. Nikolaev flying this aircraft managed to rescue his comrade, Junior Lieutenant I.T. Koloskov, whose plane was hit in air combat, and landed in enemy territory. The aircraft is painted in the colours standard for this fighter type in the first half of the war: AMT-4 green with AMT-6 black blotches on upper surfaces, and AMT-7 light blue on lower surfaces. Note the white spinner. Red stars have black trimming. The white lightning bolt on the fin over the star is the regimental recognition mark of the 88th GvIAP.

Colour views by Mikhail Bykov

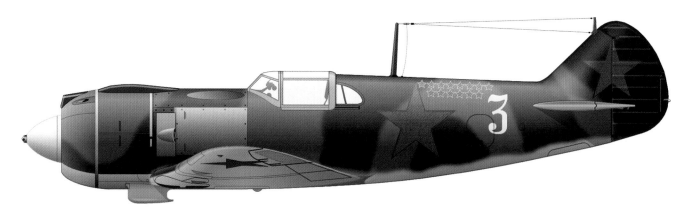

Lavochkin La-5 'White 3', 40th GvIAP

Flown by Lieutenant K.A. Novikov. This pilot scored five air victories in the course of the Belgorod defence operation. The aircraft is painted in the colours standard for this fighter type in the first half of the war: AMT-4 green with AMT-6 black blotches on upper surfaces, and AMT-7 light blue on lower surfaces. Note the white spinner, unpainted metal of the canopy framing, and red star victory marks with white trim. Red stars also have black trim.

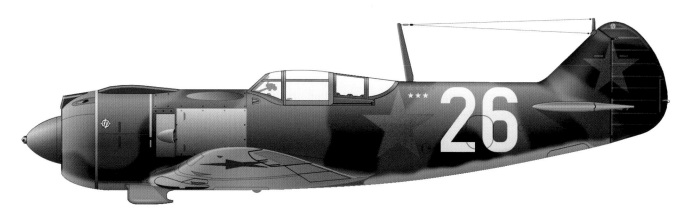

Lavochkin La-5F 'White 26', serial number 39210126, 486th IAP

Flown by Major K.A. Pelipets, Commander of the 486th IAP. He was shot down on July 5 1943 and became a POW. The aircraft is painted in the colours standard for this fighter type in the first half of the war: AMT-4 green with AMT-6 black blotches on upper surfaces, and AMT-7 light blue on lower surfaces. Note two lines of star victory marks (upper in red and lower in white). Red star insignias have no trim.

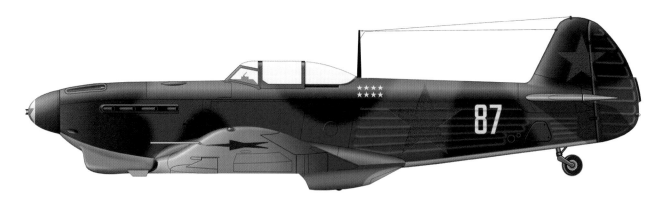

Yakolev Yak-1 'White 87', 427th IAP

Flown by Junior Lieutenant V.P. Torubalko. According to the unit's records, on 7 July this pilot scored four personal air victories and one victory when flying in a group. The aircraft is painted in the colours standard for this fighter type in the first half of the war: AMT-4 green with AMT-6 black blotches on upper surfaces, and AMT-7 light blue on lower surfaces. The propeller spinner has a red star mark on the white background on the tip. The red star victory marks on the fuselage are white. Red star insignias have no trim.

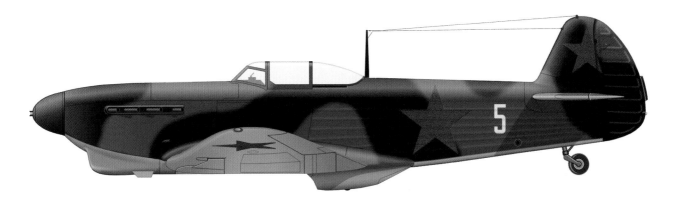

Yakolev Yak-1 'White 5', 247th IAP

Flown by Lieutenant V.M. Shevchuk. The aircraft is painted in the colours standard for this fighter type in the first half of the war: AMT-4 green with AMT-6 black blotches on upper surfaces, and AMT-7 light blue on lower surfaces. Red stars have no trim.

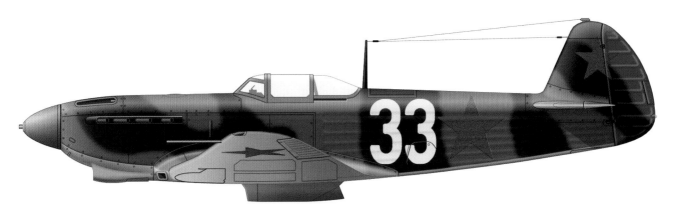

Yakolev Yak-7b 'White 33', of one of the units of the 256th IAD

The aircraft is painted in the colours standard for this fighter type in the first half of the war: AMT-4 green with AMT-6 black blotches on upper surfaces, and AMT-7 light blue on lower surfaces. Red stars have no trim.

Yakolev Yak-9 'White 4', 586th IAP, 9th IAK, Air Defence Force

Flown by female pilot Senior Lieutenant Z. Seid-Mamedova, Navigator of the 586th IAP. The aircraft is painted in the colours standard for this fighter type in the first half of the war: AMT-4 green with AMT-6 black blotches on upper surfaces, and AMT-7 light blue on lower surfaces. Red stars have black trim. Note the different shades of the camouflage blotches which possibly appeared after post-repair painting.

Colour views by Mikhail Bykov

Lavochkin La-5 'White 48', 8th GvIAD

Unknown pilot. The aircraft is painted in the colours standard for this fighter type in the first half of the war: AMT-4 green with AMT-6 black blotches on upper surfaces, and AMT-7 light blue on lower surfaces. Red stars have no trim.

Messerschmitt Bf 109G-4 'White 6', serial number 19968, 7./JG52

Flown by *Feldwebel* E. Lohberg. On 7 July he was shot down and became a POW. The fighter received standard factory camouflage of RLM 74 (*Dunkelgrau, grünlich*)/RLM 75 (*Mittelgrau*) on upper surfaces with blotches of RLM 70 (*Schwarzgrün*) and RLM 02 (*Grau*). Lower surfaces are painted in RLM 76 (*Lichtblau*). Propeller spinner is green/black RLM 70 (*Schwarzgrün*).

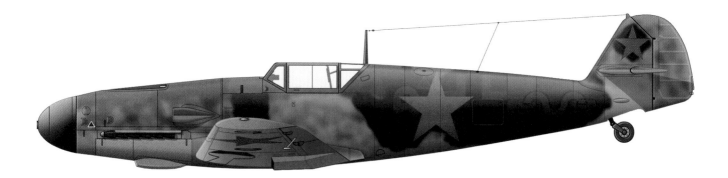

Messerschmitt Bf 109G-4, serial number 19968

The captured machine was tested at the Scientific Testing Institute of the Air Force in September–October 1943. The fighter had standard factory camouflage of RLM 74 (*Dunkelgrau, grünlich*)/RLM 75 (*Mittelgrau*) on upper surfaces with blotches of RLM 70 (*Schwarzgrün*) and RLM 02 (*Grau*). Lower surfaces are painted in RLM 76 (*Lichtblau*). After capture the German identification marks and insignias were painted over with blotches of AMT-6 black, and red star markings (with no trim) were applied.

Colour views by Mikhail Bykov

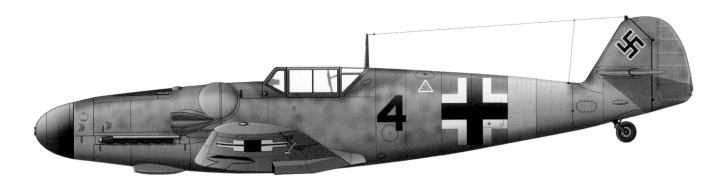

Messerschmitt Bf 109G-6 'Black 4', I./JG52

Flown by *Oberfeldwebel* R. Trenkel. The fighter had standard factory camouflage of RLM 74 (*Dunkelgrau, grünlich*)/RLM 75 (*Mittelgrau*) on upper surfaces with blotches of RLM 70 (*Schwarzgrün*) and RLM 02 (*Grau*). Lower surfaces are painted in RLM 76 (*Lichtblau*). Propeller spinner is combination of green/black RLM 70 (*Schwarzgrün*) and dark red.

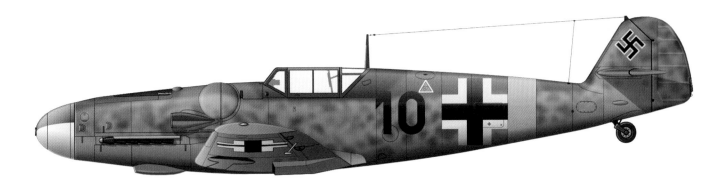

Messerschmitt Bf 109G-6 'Black 10', I./JG52

The fighter had standard factory camouflage of RLM 74 (*Dunkelgrau, grünlich*)/RLM 75 (*Mittelgrau*) on upper surfaces with blotches of RLM 70 (*Schwarzgrün*) and RLM 02 (*Grau*). Lower surfaces are painted in RLM 76 (*Lichtblau*). Propeller spinner is combination of green/black RLM 70 (*Schwarzgrün*) and white.

Messerschmitt Bf 109G-4 'Yellow 6', serial number 14940, II./JG3

Flown by *Feldwebel* A. Fischer. He was shot down on the eve of Operation 'Zitadelle'. The fighter had standard factory camouflage of RLM 74 (*Dunkelgrau, grünlich*)/RLM 75 (*Mittelgrau*) on upper surfaces with blotches of RLM 70 (*Schwarzgrün*) and RLM 02 (*Grau*). Lower surfaces are painted in RLM 76 (*Lichtblau*). Propeller spinner is combination of green/black RLM 70 (*Schwarzgrün*) and yellow.

Colour views by Mikhail Bykov

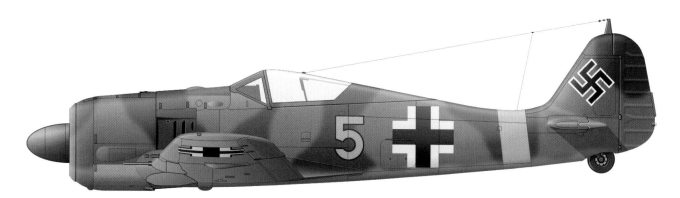

Focke Wulf Fw 190A-4 'Yellow 5', I./JG51, July 1943

Flown by *Feldwebel* J. Jennewein. The fighter had a camouflage of RLM 70 (*Schwarzgrün*)/RLM 79 (*Sandgelb*) on upper surfaces. Lower surfaces are painted in RLM 76 (*Lichtblau*). Propeller spinner is green/black RLM 70 (*Schwarzgrün*).

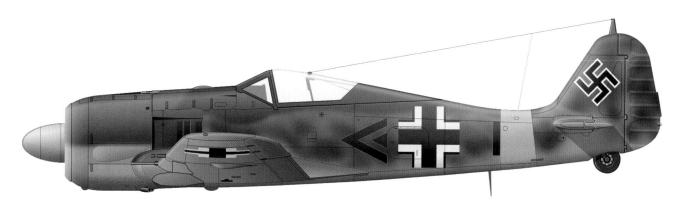

Focke Wulf Fw 190A-5, III./JG51

Flown by the commander of III./JG51, *Hauptmann* F. Losigkeit. The fighter had standard factory camouflage of RLM 74 (*Dunkelgrau, grünlich*)/RLM 75 (*Mittelgrau*) on upper surfaces with blotches of RLM 70 (*Schwarzgrün*) and RLM 02 (*Grau*). Lower surfaces are painted in RLM 76 (*Lichtblau*). Propeller spinner is yellow.

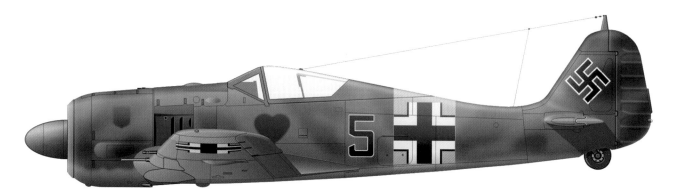

Focke Wulf Fw 190A-4 'Black 5', 2/JG54

Flown by one of the high-scoring aces of the *Grünherz Geschwader*, *Kommandeur* of the 2/JG54 *Oberleutnant* H. Götz. The fighter had a camouflage of RLM 70 (*Schwarzgrün*)/ RLM 71 (*Dunkelgrün*) on upper surfaces. Lower surfaces are painted in RLM 76 (*Lichtblau*). Propeller spinner is RLM 70 (*Schwarzgrün*).

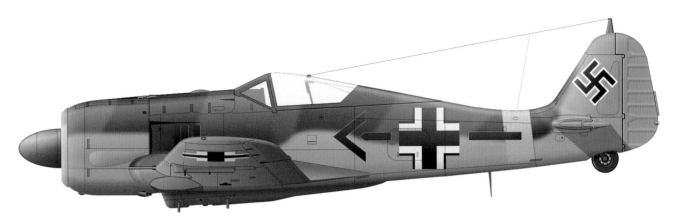

Focke Wulf Fw 190F-3, SchG1

Flown by *Geschwaderkommodore* SchG1 *Major* A. Druschel. The fighter had a camouflage of RLM 74 (*Dunkelgrau, grünlich*)/RLM 75 (*Mittelgrau*) on upper surfaces. Lower surfaces are painted in RLM 76 (*Lichtblau*). Propeller spinner is RLM 70 (*Schwarzgrün*).

Focke Wulf Fw 190F-3 'Red G', II./SchG1

The airplane was received from the Arado factory right before the battle. The fighter had standard factory camouflage of RLM 74 (*Dunkelgrau, grünlich*)/RLM 75 (*Mittelgrau*) on upper surfaces with blotches of RLM 70 (*Schwarzgrün*) and RLM 02 (*Grau*). Lower surfaces are painted in RLM 76 (*Lichtblau*). Propeller spinner is a combination of RLM 70 (*Schwarzgrün*) and dark red with white trimming.

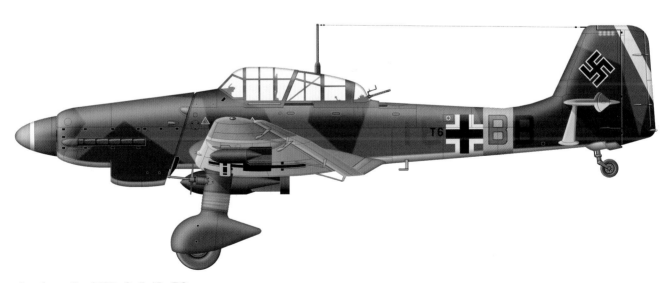

Junkers Ju 87D-3, I./StG2

The aircraft is camouflaged in a combination of RLM 70 (*Schwarzgrün*) and RLM 71 (*Dunkelgrün*) colours on upper surfaces. Lower surfaces are painted in RLM 65 (*Hellbrau* of 1941 standard). Propeller spinner is green with white band.

Colour views by Mikhail Bykov

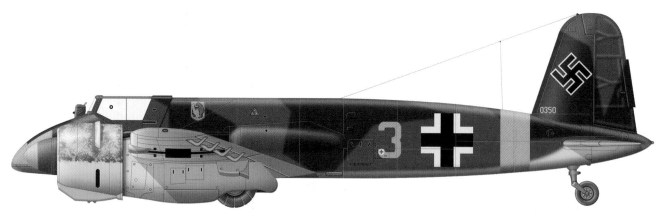

Henschel Hs 129B-2 'Yellow 3', *Panzerjägerstaffel* JG51

The aircraft is camouflaged in a combination of RLM 70 (*Schwarzgrün*) and RLM 71 (*Dunkelgrün*) colours on upper surfaces. Lower surfaces are painted in RLM 65 (*Hellbrau* of 1941 standard). Propeller spinner tips are yellow. Note the remains of the temporary winter camouflage on the upper sides of engine cowlings.

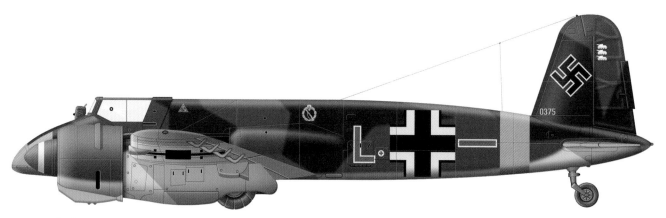

Henschel Hs 129B-2 'Red L', serial number 0375, 8./SchG1

The aircraft is camouflaged in a combination of RLM 70 (*Schwarzgrün*) and RLM 71 (*Dunkelgrün*) colours on upper surfaces. Lower surfaces are painted in RLM 65 (*Hellbrau* of 1941 standard). Propeller spinner tips are red with White band.

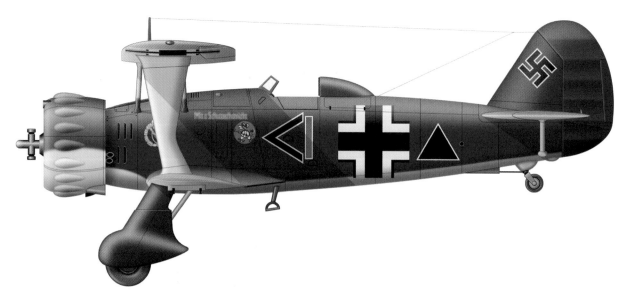

Henschel Hs 129B, 7./SchG1

Flown by the commander of 7./SchG1, *Hauptmann* J. Menapace. The aircraft is camouflaged in a combination of RLM 70 (*Schwarzgrün*) and RLM 71 (*Dunkelgrün*) colours on upper surfaces. Lower surfaces are painted in RLM 65 (*Hellbrau* of 1941 standard).

Illyushin Il-2 'White 37' of the 820th ShAP

On 5 July the aircraft received considerable damage from German flak, but returned to the Grinev airfield. The aircraft is painted in the colours standard for this type in the first half of the war: AMT-4 green with AMT-6 black blotches on upper surfaces, and AMT-7 light blue on lower surfaces. Note fuzzy edges of the camouflage blotches. Red stars have no trim.

Douglas Boston III Black 64 / 'Red 1' which belonged to a unit of the 244th BAD

The aircraft carries British bomber camouflage pattern: Dark Green and Dark Earth on top with Sky undersides. Red stars have black trim.

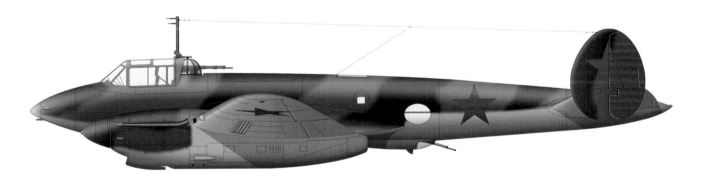

Petlyakov Pe-2 'Red 4', 81st BAP

Flown by Lieutenant N.I. Gapeenok. The aircraft is painted in the colours standard for this type in the first half of the war: AMT-4 green with AMT-6 black blotches on upper surfaces, and AMT-7 light blue on lower surfaces. Red stars have no trim.

Colour views by Mikhail Bykov

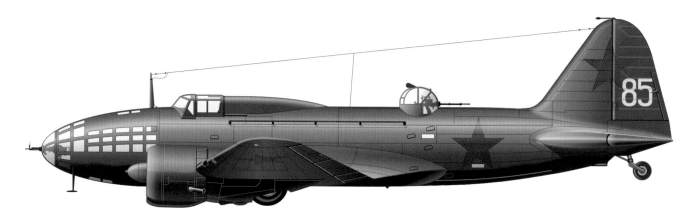

Illyushin Il-2 'White 85', Long-Range Aviation unit, July 1943

The aircraft is painted in AMT-4 green on upper surfaces with AMT-6 black undersides. Red stars have no trim.

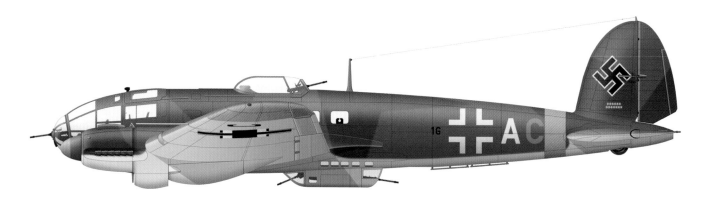

Heinkel He 111-16, II./KG27

The aircraft is camouflaged in combination of RLM 70 (*Schwarzgrün*) and RLM 71 (*Dunkelgrün*) colours on upper surfaces. Lower surfaces are painted in RLM 65 (*Hellbrau* of 1941 standard). Propeller spinner tips are bright green.

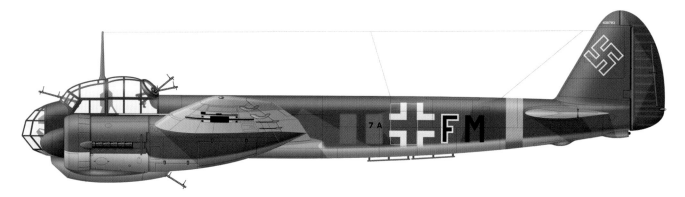

Junkers Ju 88D-1, serial number 430783, 4(F)/121

This aircraft received considerable damage from Soviet anti-aircraft artillery in the vicinity of Kursk. The aircraft is camouflaged in a combination of RLM 70 (*Schwarzgrün*) and RLM 71 (*Dunkelgrün*) colours on upper surfaces. Lower surfaces are painted in RLM 65 (*Hellbrau* of 1941 standard).

U-2 'White 26', unidentified unit, July 1943

The aircraft is painted in AMT-4 green on upper surfaces with AMT-7 light blue undersides.

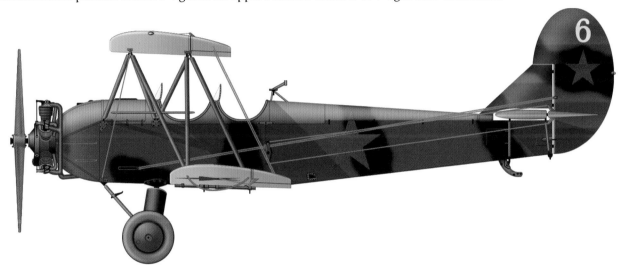

U-2 'White 6', 271st NBAD

The aircraft received combat damage in a mission on the first night of the defence battle, but was rapidly restored and returned to action. The aircraft is painted in AMT-4 green with AMT-6 black blotches on upper surfaces, and AMT-7 light blue on lower surfaces.

Heinkel He 46C 'White 14', which belonged to 1. *Behelfskampfstaffel Luftflotte* 4

The aircraft is camouflaged in a combination of RLM 70 (*Schwarzgrün*) and RLM 71 (*Dunkelgrün*) colours on upper surfaces. Lower surfaces are painted in RLM 65 (*Hellbrau* of 1941 standard).

Colour views by Mikhail Bykov

Chapter 3
Breakthrough to Kursk

Under a plan, developed by the Soviet command, Soviet aviation was to deliver a pre-emptive attack on the enemy on the southern sector of the Kursk area. As a result, the very first day of the battle turned out to be very unusual – it was the first Soviet large-scale defensive operation to start with massive air strikes against enemy airfields. In exact compliance with the plan, several groups of attack aircraft from the 2nd and the 17th Air Armies took off at dawn to deliver air strikes against seven large German airfields. According to reconnaissance, some of the airfields accommodated up to 150 aircraft, and if the operation went as planned, the *Luftwaffe* strength would be undermined considerably. Assets allocated for the air strikes were quite significant. Each air army was to send sixty-six Il-2s, and a great number of escort fighters. General S.A. Krasovskiy's subordinates were to attack enemy airfields outside Belgorod (Sokolniki, Pomerki, and

⋔ Loading the Il-2.

⋔ An Il-2 ground attack aircraft in action.

⋓ Sergeant N.M. Skomorokhov from the 164th IAP (later a Marshal of Aviation, and twice HSU) in the cabin of his La-5 after a sortie.

⋔ Soviet troops observing the progress of air combat.

With his sunshade in place, this *Unteroffizier* from 4./JG3 awaits the signal for take-off.

A Heinkel He 111 from KG27 on a combat heading.

A technician from *Stab* SG1 relaxes beside an Fw 190 with his toolbox beside his head.

Despite sustaining severe flak damage, this Il-2 from the 820th ShAP managed to land at Grinyev airfield some 70km east of Belgorod.

Mikoyanovks), while pilots from V.A. Sudets' unit were to strike airfields outside Kharkov (Rogan and Osnova). In addition, the 17th Air Army also allocated aircraft to attack the Barvenkovo and the Kramatorskaya airfields. A total of 417 aircraft were expected to be engaged in the small hours of the morning and on the previous night at least sixty Yakolev and Lavochkin fighters from the 2nd Air Army were also detailed to intercept any German fighters.

An unusual beginning

The Soviet command gambled on the fact that the *Luftwaffe* would not be able to scramble most of its fighters in time, and any German patrols would be intercepted by the powerful fighter escort. In addition to that, attack aircraft from the 2nd and the 17th Air Armies were expected to approach their targets 'down-sun' from the east, which would make it difficult for German air defence gunners to aim their weapons. Such assumptions may have been reasonable, but modern German tactics foiled any surprise element. Large groups of Messerschmitts were waiting for the Soviet aircraft

on the approaches to their targets and had been warned by crews of the Freya and the Würzburg radars, which had been operating outside Belgorod and Kharkov since spring 1943, and each radar was capable of detecting an individual aircraft at a range of 80–90 km, and large groups at a range of 130–150 km. Soviet reconnaissance was well aware this, but the commanding officers did not pay due attention to the fact.

It should also be taken into account that most *Luftwaffe* units, especially fighter units, were ready to scramble immediately as they complied strictly with orders to stay on high alert, issued right before Operation 'Zitadelle'. Most flight crews from the 8th Air Corps had arrived at airfields, and aircraft had been armed and fuelled even before dawn. *General* H. Plocher noted in his report on the events, which unfolded at German airfields on the morning of 5 July: "Messerschmitts from Squadrons JG3 and JG52 took off without waiting for the bombers to arrive, as had been planned in advance. They intercepted approaching squadrons of Soviet aircraft in the grey mist of the early dawn. In the course of ensuing air engagements most

⋂ Captain G.S. Glinkin from the 5th GvIAP, 17th VA in the cabin of his La-5.

German pilots managed to score quite a few victories, increasing their personal scores considerably. The Russians operated in their invariable unoriginal formations, but they demonstrated their usual stubbornness and self-sacrifice by keeping their combat formations steady. They lost most of their aircraft which took part in the air strike. The air battle, which broke out at a relatively low altitude, could be observed from the ground, which was also facilitated by the lack of clouds. The German defenders demonstrated a doubtless superiority over the attackers. Such large-scale air engagements were rare for the Eastern Front, and the neighbouring terrain was soon covered with the debris of Soviet bombers (in fact, the air strike was delivered by Il-2 attack aircraft – author) and escort fighters. Chief of the *Luftwaffe* General Staff *General* H. Jeschonnek, who was at the forward command post of the 8th Air Corps, personally saw the defeat of the Soviets."

Plocher's account was echoed by the Commander of the 8th Air Corps *General* H. Seidemann who said: "We witnessed an unusual sight – burning and falling aircraft left their traces all over the sky. A total of about 120 Russian aircraft were destroyed within a short period of time. Our own losses were insignificant, which allowed us to claim a total victory in the air battle." At the same time Seidemann stated that he and General Jeschonnek, as well as escort officers, had faced a couple of uneasy moments, when an armada of 400–500 enemy aircraft, flying in tight combat formations, had crossed the front line. Soviet reports clarify some of the details of the air strike and first it is worth mentioning that in fact a total of about 250 aircraft and fighters (excluding aircraft tasked with intercepting enemy fighters) took part in the attacks on the German airfields and in addition to

⋂ *Oberleutnant* J. Kirschner from II./JG52 interrogates a captured Soviet pilot.

that, not every group reached its target at full strength – for instance, only six of twelve Il-2s from the 735th ShAP, the 266th ShAD, took off for reasons unknown. The strength of the strike unit soon dwindled to four aircraft – one of the aircraft lost the group north-west of Kharkov when approaching the target, and another carried out an emergency landing in friendly territory due to an engine failure.

A dozen attack aircraft from the 66th ShAP, flying a slight distance away, had also suffered losses over the airfield when two Il-2s had collided in mid-air. Thus, only eighteen of twenty-four aircraft from the 266th ShAD took off, and of those only fourteen reached their target. The 2nd Air Army lost twenty attack aircraft, and the 17th Air Army lost about fifteen in the morning air strikes. The 237th ShAP, the 305th ShAD of the Air Army, commanded by Sudets, and tasked with delivering air strikes against the Rogan and Kharkov-Osnova airfields, suffered the most tragic fate. Realising possible problems, divisional commanding officer Lieutenant Colonel N.G. Mikhevichev reinforced Major Karbinskiy's group with seasoned pilots from other regiments, though it did little to help as huge losses were suffered during strikes against airfields outside Kharkov. Attacks mounted by flight crews from the 17th Air Army on Barvenkovo and Kramatorskaya airfields, although not seeing any heavy losses, did not see any significant results. Some groups failed to reach their targets due to adverse weather and dropped their bombs on secondary targets, while other aircraft groups bombed dummies, set up by the Germans on the outskirts of the airfields in advance. Meanwhile, fighter squadrons from the 27th IAP and the 40th IAP returning from their missions unexpectedly came across numerous large groups of German aircraft, flying towards the front line. They were the forerunners of the battle, breaking out on the southern sector of the Kursk area.

The air battle unfolds

Soviet artillery had conducted counter-preparation at the Voronezh Front twice before dawn and the results turned out to be more significant than those at the Central Front. According to Soviet documents, preparatory bombardments suppressed dozens of enemy artillery batteries and destroyed seventeen observation posts and it took the German command several hours to restore the damage, especially to communications. From the very outset the Germans started their breakthrough in the defensive area of the 6th Guards Army, headed by General I.M. Chistyakov. Here the army faced five tank, one motorised, and two infantry divisions (from the 2nd SS Panzer Corps, the 48th Panzer Corps, and the 52nd Army Corps). The peculiar feature of the German task force consisted of the fact that it was clearly short of infantry and artillery for breaching well-organised and well-equipped defensive positions, thus the role of *Luftwaffe* presence increased dramatically which was highlighted at dawn on July 5 when the 4th Air Fleet launched extremely massive attacks, as Soviet VNOS observation posts registered in excess of 400 enemy combat sorties within the first hour of the battle alone.

Army Group South demonstrated a stronger will and persistence in fulfilling the offensive plan and in addition to that, the attack against Soviet troops mounted from outside Belgorod was more powerful since Manstein had more support, including tank units, than von Kluge. Besides, the terrain on the southern

↻ The smouldering remains of a Messerschmitt aircraft, seen in the Voronezh Front sector during July.

sector of the Orel-Kursk area favoured employment of large mechanised forces and aviation by both sides; it was far more difficult for General N.F. Vatutin to guess enemy plans. On the Voronezh Front the enemy dealt several especially powerful blows in the wide front-line sector in Oboyan and Korocha by throwing large tank units into action, while the Supreme High Command General Headquarters and the General Staff believed that the enemy had concentrated a more powerful force in the Central Front. The offensive, mounted by Army Group South, featured a high coordination of all combat arms and intensive employment of every weapon system. Tank and infantry attacks were accompanied by massive air strikes and groups of fifty to one hundred and twenty He 111s from KG27, KG55, and I./KG100, took out airfields outside Kharkov, and Ju 88s from KG3 took out Poltava airfield, and delivered fierce bomb strikes against Soviet troops outside Syrtsev, Gertsovka, and Ternovka. It soon became clear that a 15km long defensive area between Butovo and Dragunskoe defended by the 67th and the 52nd Rifle Divisions, came under the most powerful attack as a total of up to 2,000 German combat sorties were registered over that area within a single day.

In the first half of the day the German command eased combat missions by detailing groups of two and four Messerschmitts to patrol the probable approaches

⋂ Army General N.F. Vatutin, Commander of Voronezh front sector in a trench.

⋃ A number of German captured airmen seen in early July in the Belgorod sector.

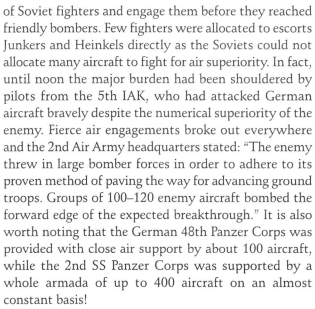

○ Technicians prepare this Henschel Hs 129B ground-attack aircraft – note the 30mm Mk.103 cannon beneath the fuselage.

○ Ju 87 Stukas head towards their target.

of Soviet fighters and engage them before they reached friendly bombers. Few fighters were allocated to escorts Junkers and Heinkels directly as the Soviets could not allocate many aircraft to fight for air superiority. In fact, until noon the major burden had been shouldered by pilots from the 5th IAK, who had attacked German aircraft bravely despite the numerical superiority of the enemy. Fierce air engagements broke out everywhere and the 2nd Air Army headquarters stated: "The enemy threw in large bomber forces in order to adhere to its proven method of paving the way for advancing ground troops. Groups of 100–120 enemy aircraft bombed the forward edge of the expected breakthrough." It is also worth noting that the German 48th Panzer Corps was provided with close air support by about 100 aircraft, while the 2nd SS Panzer Corps was supported by a whole armada of up to 400 aircraft on an almost constant basis!

The 6 x 4km defensive area of the 52nd Guards Rifle Division saw non-stop air strikes for 15 hours! Heroic actions of an air defence battery from the 1357th Small-Calibre Air Defence Artillery Regiment, which protected the division, could not save the situation and it was not surprising that the divisional defences were

breached and overrun by German tanks and mechanised infantry at about noon.

Meanwhile, the Soviet strike aircraft had managed to put themselves in order after the morning air strikes, went into action as well. The 291st ShAD operated efficiently and managed to halt the German 48th Panzer Corps. As already mentioned above, the Soviet command prepared quite a number of 'surprises' for the enemy in spring and early summer, with one of them being the new PTAB-2.5-1.5 shaped-charge air bombs, and in order to capitalise on the element of surprise to the fullest extent it was decided to employ these new bombs massively, and on the orders of the Supreme High Command General Headquarters only. It would be safe to state that pilots from the 61st ShAP, the 291st ShAD, were the first to employ new PTAB-2.5-1.5 shaped-charge bombs on the morning of 5 July when a group of Il-2s, led by Senior Lieutenant Dobkevich, managed to deliver a surprise air strike against an enemy convoy outside a village of Butovo.

When recovering from run-ins, flight crews saw a great number of burning tanks and other vehicles and when retreating from the target, the group also successfully repulsed Messerschmitt attacks, shooting down one of them and taking its pilot as a prisoner of war. The divisional command decided to capitalise on the success, and air strikes delivered by aircraft from the 61st ShAP were followed by more attacks by groups from the 241st and the 617th regiments. Pilots reported killing up to fifteen enemy tanks and the use of the new bombs did not come unnoticed by the Voronezh Front command. General Vatutin noted in his night report to Stalin: "A group of eight Il-2s bomb concentrated enemy tanks with the help of new bombs. The efficiency of the bomb strike was high: twelve enemy tanks were set on fire immediately."

Colonel A.N. Vitruk's subordinates, who operated bravely and competently as far as tactics were concerned, made it considerably harder for German tank units to discharge their tasks. The *Großdeutschland* Division, facing artillery bombardment and air strikes, failed to negotiate the rain-eroded terrain which was literally stuffed with minefields, and blew up a total of twenty-five tanks. Thus, the Germans felt the power of Soviet air strikes from the very outset of the battle on the southern sector of the Kursk area. The description of this combat episode, given by Chief of Staff of the 48th Corps General von Mellentin, is well-known:

"Russian pilots demonstrated exceptional valour in the course of this battle, despite German air superiority." German fighters had changed their tactics by noon. They now operated in large groups of between twenty to fifty aircraft attempting to intercept Soviet aircraft on the approaches to the front line. On most occasions they succeeded and were able to seize the initiative and a total of about fifty Soviet aircraft were lost to simultaneous attacks from various directions!

The 1st ShAK suffered the heaviest losses on 5 July loosing thirty-two Il-2s. Flights crews from the 1st BAK, operating at an altitude of 2,300–2,900m outside Butovo and Pushkarnoe survived several intensive air engagements with Messerschmitts and a combat sortie, carried out by flight crews from the 854th BAP, the 293rd BAD, turned out to be failure when Bf 109s from I./JG52 shot down six of nine Pe-2s, and another Pe-2 fell victim to air defence artillery fire. No one could have guessed that the 1st BAK would carry out its next combat sortie only on 12 July; such a long break was caused by the necessity to involve fighters from the 4th IAK in battling for air superiority and the inability to provide I.S. Polbin's bombers with reliable protection against enemy fighters. The results

↻ *Hauptmann* J. Vise, acting I./JG52 *Gruppekommandeur* was credited with the destruction of twelve Soviet aircraft on 5 July.

↻ *Generalfeldmarschall* E. Manstein with his officers.

achieved by the 1st BAK on 5 July are as follows: a total of 115 combat sorties resulted in destroying forty houses, five tanks, and about forty motorcars. The most successful hit was scored against a concentration of motorcars outside Berezovka and a fuel depot south-west of Butovo, which blew up in a powerful explosion.

Soviet forces held their ground firmly, however, and many senior German officers were still sure of the final outcome, which is confirmed by the interrogation of the Ju 88D flight crew from 2(F)/11, shot down by Sergeant Omelchenko from the 183rd IAP at an altitude of 7,000m outside Alekseevka. Captured German *Leutnant* H. Schulz stated that his crew had been ordered to monitor the retreat of Soviet units from the area north and east of Belgorod towards Korocha, Novyi Oskol, and Oboyan. However, they did not see any retreat. According to the 2nd Air Army headquarters, fighters from the 8th Guards IAD, the 5th IAK, achieved the greatest success that day by shooting down seventy-six (!) enemy aircraft. Senior Lieutenant N.D. Gulaev and Senior Lieutenant I.N. Shpak from the 27th IAP, Senior Lieutenant O.V. Belikov from the 88th Guards IAP, and Senior Lieutenant M.S. Vanin from the 41st Guards IAP scored four combat victories each, although according to Soviet sources, the 2nd Air Army lost eighty-three aircraft, and another fifty were damaged.

In turn, the *Luftwaffe* Quartermaster-General reported that the 8th Air Corps had fifty-eight aircraft non-operational with twenty-five destroyed and seven more aircraft to be scrapped. This data is incomplete, since it does not take into account all the losses sustained by Group I./JG52. German fighters initially claimed 303 air victories, but German headquarters reduced the figure to 220 later. A total of forty more Soviet aircraft were considered to have been shot down by air defence artillery. Naturally, victories claimed were not divided equally among German pilots, and some of the aces turned out to have achieved really phenomenal results (Table 4).

German sources state that Group II./JG3 conducted seventy-seven successful air engagements and on the first day of the battle JG52 *Commodore Oberstleutnant* D. Hrabak undertook three successful dogfights, while StG2 commander *Major* E. Kupfer conducted his 600th combat sortie. Although, the Germans did not report

⋂ Pe-2 bombers en-route to their target

victories alone they do not deny the fact that a number of leading fighter pilots were killed or wounded on the first day of Operation 'Zitadelle'. Suffice to say that the commander of the headquarters flight of Group III./JG3 *Hauptmann* L. Eggers was killed in a dogfight south-west of Belgorod as early as the morning of 5 July whilst *Hauptmann* J. Wiese, the most efficient German ace of that day, made five emergency landings that day. Group III./JG52 suffered the heaviest and most irreplaceable losses with up to ten of its Messerschmitts and six pilots killed and wounded, including three expert fighter pilots. *Oberleutnant* W. Krupinski had to stay in hospital for over a month after an unsuccessful emergency landing, and *Feldwebel* K. Schumacher (fifty-six air victories) bailing out of a burning aircraft was also heavily wounded, *Feldwebel* W. Hauswirth (fifty-

No.	Rank	Name	Unit	Number of victories
1	Hauptmann	J. Wiese	I/JG52	12
2	Oberleutnant	W. Krupinski	III/JG52	11
3	Oberleutnant	J. Kirschner	II/JG3	9
4	Feldwebel	H. Gruenberg	II/JG3	7
5	Oberleutnant	W. Bitsch	III/JG3	6

✚ **Table 4: Efficiency of the best German pilots on 5 July 1943**

◑ Junior Lieutenant S.M. Liskin and Lieutenant N.I. Galeyonok (later HSU) discussing a recent sortie in front of a Pe-2.

four victories) was killed in a dogfight north-east of Kharkov and *Unteroffizier* M. Lotzmann (fifteen victories) was reported missing in action.

The German offensive continues

The distinctive feature of aviation employment in the Soviet-German front consisted in its close coordination with battles fought on the ground. The battle on the southern sector of the Kursk area was not an exception in this regard. Groups of German aircraft, each comprising 12–15 dive-bombers and eight to ten fighters, appeared over the battlefield as soon as ground troops resumed the offensive. Junkers bombed Soviet infantry and artillery positions in steep dives in an attempt to facilitate the advance of their own tanks. The German command, which had never before encountered so many air defence guns and machine guns of various calibres on the battlefield, attached much importance to destroying such weapons and their crews during the July offensive. If the enemy was not able to augment its air strikes on air defence artillery firing positions with artillery or mortar bombardments, it delivered numerous air strikes against such positions. Fw 190s from SchG1 were widely employed to strafe and drop small high-explosive bombs on Soviet firing positions.

According to German recollections, subordinates of *Major* A. Druschel were stunned by the actions of Red Army soldiers during air strikes delivered by Focke-Wulfs. While *Wehrmacht* soldiers immediately flopped into the mud on seeing enemy aircraft, allowing the air defence gunners to deal with the enemy aviation, Soviet soldiers "all started firing anything that could be fired at German aircraft!" One of the attack aircraft pilots recalled later on: "The Russians opened dense and non-stop fire from assault rifles, rifles, and even pistols. The density of fire in the air exceeded any level imaginable. I believe that if the Russians had been able to tear horseshoes off their horses at that moment, they would have tried to hit our aircraft with them as well!" According to Soviet reports, active resistance to German aviation with the help of both organic and non-organic air defence weapons had been prepared long before the outset of Operation 'Zitadelle'. For instance, the Voronezh Front had prepared a total of 2,132 rifle groups, 1,551 light and 829 heavy machine guns, 2,169 anti-tank rifles, and fifty field guns for engaging enemy aircraft.

Meanwhile, the 2nd Air Army headquarters was not able to focus aviation efforts on the main axis of enemy advance; only 309 of 1,078 combat sorties made on 6 July resulted in attacking enemy tanks and infantry. Attack aircraft were the major strike force and they approached the forward edge of the battle area in echelon formation of six or eight aircraft under a fighter escort and attacked from an altitude of 800–1,200m in shallow dives. First, they machine-gunned their targets, then launched rocket projectiles, dropped bombs at an altitude of 500–600 m, and fired VYa cannon at an altitude of 300m. The 291st ShAD attacked the enemy with a similar intensity; six massive air strikes involved eighty-two Il-2s and 122 fighters. On 6 July the 2nd Air Army lost twenty-two Il-2s, and the following day it lost thirteen more aircraft. General S.A. Khudyakov, a representative of the Supreme High Command General Headquarters, reported: "The decision to change aviation tactics, adopted the day before, which envisioned massive employment of large groups of aircraft, turned out to be absolutely correct. The Voronezh Front command deemed aviation activities to be considerably more efficient than the day before." As early as July 7 it became obvious that in addition to 'free hunting', the enemy had also reinforced the protection of its own attack aircraft, which were now escorted by fighters to the target and back.

The situation in the Oboyan area worsened for Soviet forces with each passing hour. Despite all the steps taken, the German Panzer corps continued breaching the Soviet defences systematically every day and on the night of 8 July N.F. Vatutin decided to fulfil the long-planned counter-attack, involving five tank corps, which was expected to result in drastic changes in the Voronezh Front. Unfortunately, preparation for the counter-attack could not have been worse. Despite the fact that the order on mounting an offensive was dated 23:00 hours of 7 July, corps commanding officers received it only the following morning and did not have time to respond, and some units were on the move to a staging area and lagged two to three hours behind the planned schedule. Despite this the front commander did not postpone the offensive, which resulted in the subsequent failure of the counter-attack.

Meanwhile, after getting the latest air reconnaissance data, the German 4th Panzer Army command launched its own offensive in the north-western direction, forestalling the Soviet troops by a mere half an hour. This was the first time Hs 129B attack aircraft, armed with 30mm ventral cannon, had appeared in the sky, and although the Hs 129B, powered by two obsolete low-power French Gnome-Rhone engines, was not the best aircraft it was quite a stable platform for its gun armament and boasted excellent protection of the pilot. Soviet tanks were attacked by such detachments from Jg.Pz./JG51, 4(Pz.)/SchG1, 8(Pz.)/SchG1, and 4(Pz.)/SchG2 under the overall command of *Capitan* B. Meyer. *General* H. Plocher wrote in his book '*Luftwaffe* Against Russia' "Soviet tank units unexpectedly crossed the Donets and the Belgorod-Kursk railway, and approached the offensive sector of the 2nd SS Panzer Corps in an attempt to mount a flank attack, but the 8th Air Corps had thrown into action four tank-killing detachments, each equipped with about sixteen Hs 129 aircraft. The detachments took successive turns in attacking the

◖ A German armoured column moves towards the front line. Note the Swastika flag draped over the vehicles to identify them as a friendly force from the air.

◗ The 'scoreboard' of II./JG3, as seen during the *Unternehmen Zitadelle*.

♙ A Henschel Hs 129B being prepared.

Russians. And the 'killing wheel' of the 8th Corps operated for about an hour, after which surviving Russians took cover in the woods."

On 8 July some units of the 17th Air Army took part in combat operations in the Oboyan direction to step up pressure on the enemy, however, Soviet aircraft did not manage to achieve any significant success there due to poor knowledge of the area by the pilots, remoteness of the battle area from their home bases, and the lack of ground guidance. According to reports of the 2nd Air Army, on 8 July aircraft from the 1st ShAK and the 291st ShAD operated in groups of eighteen to twenty aircraft and ten to twelve fighters respectively. Attack aircraft made a total of 520 combat sorties, destroying and damaging dozens of enemy tanks and motorcars. German fighters conducted a total of thirty-seven air engagements shooting down twenty-five Il-2s and six escort fighters. The best German fighter pilots continued hunting Soviet aircraft and most of the thirty-five lost on 9 July fell prey to such 'free hunters', with the 5th IAK alone losing eleven aircraft.

The 27th IAP experienced a bad day as well, as the enemy shot down four of its Yak-1s, including the aircraft piloted by Major A.V. Volkov, a squadron leader. A large group of Bf 109s unexpectedly appeared out of nowhere, when a group of ten Yak-1s, lead by Captain P.I. Chepinoga, was attacking a dozen Ju 87s, escorted by four Messerschmitts. The German aircraft broke up the

formation and shot down three Soviet aircraft. One of the Yak-1s shot down was piloted by Junior Lieutenant I.N. Shpak, a hero of the first day of the hostilities, who shielded his leader with his own aircraft saving the latter from certain death. However, the *Luftwaffe* Quartermaster General listed twenty-eight German aircraft from the 8th Air Corps, and two more aircraft from the 4th Air Fleet destroyed on damaged on 9 July. Squadron StG2 Immelmann lost five Ju 87 Stuka's, with four of them crashing to the ground behind the front line. Group 7./JG52 lost five Bf 109Gs with three pilots taken prisoner of war and another one wounded. *Oberfeldwebel* E. Rossmann, decorated with the Knight's Cross, and holder of ninety-three victories, was among German pilots killed or reported missing in action.

Points across the Severskiy Donets

As is known, the German 3rd Panzer Corps and part of the 11th Air Corps mounted a supporting attack in the Korocha direction south-east of Belgorod in order to protect the flank of the advancing 4th Panzer Army. On the morning of July 5 German forward units crossed the Severskiy Donets River and launched several pontoon bridges successfully. When the Voronezh Front command started receiving information that enemy tanks were crossing to the eastern bank of the river, it ordered the 3rd SAK and the 9th SAK of the 17th Air Army to destroy the pontoon bridges, as well as enemy manpower and armour. However, the decision was taken too late as about 100 German tanks had crossed the river and began mounting an offensive.

Meanwhile, efforts also focused on an area outside Bezlyudovka, Ivanovka, and Solomino, where small detachments from the 290th, the 305th, and the 306th ShADs took turns in attacking enemy crossing points. As a result of almost non-stop air strikes, attack aircraft from the 3rd SAK, which made a total of sixty-eight combat sorties, claimed to have destroyed two crossing points and up to forty enemy vehicles. Il-2s from the 9th SAK carried out 107 more combat sorties, also claiming to have destroyed two crossing points and several ammunition dumps. Nevertheless, attack aircraft from the 17th Air Army, which made about 200 combat sorties, failed to prevent units of the German 3rd Panzer Corps from crossing the Severskiy Donets. Il-2s suffered extremely heavy losses to Messerschmitts and heavy flak; suffice to say that the 290th ShAD alone lost between sixteen to thirty-two Il-2s carrying out such combat missions.

The 305th and the 306th ShADs, the 9th SAK, sustained even greater losses, losing twenty-eight aircraft and nineteen flight crews respectively! Thus the combat capabilities of Soviet attack aviation of the South-Western Front were significantly curbed on the very first day of the battle as the coordinated actions of German air defence forces resulted in reducing the combat strength of certain units of the 17th Air Army down to a third of their original strength. For instance, after two days of hostilities the 306th ShAD had only thirty-four Il-2s left, i.e. a single full-fledged regiment! At the same time, the efficiency of the Soviet air strikes turned out to be rather low – on July 6 flight crews from the 290th ShAD were the only ones to report direct hits of FAB-100s and FAB-250s at the crossing point outside Bezlyudovka.

On a number of occasions attack aircraft delivered several successful air strikes against the enemy, which are accounted for in letters of commendation from ground troops. In particular, the 17th Air Army headquarters received the following telegram: "The commanding officer of the 7th Guards Army and the commanders of the 81st and the 73rd Guards Rifle Divisions would like to express their gratitude to flight crews, which bombed enemy tanks outside Yastrebovo and Belovskaya from 15:00 until 16:00 hours on July 7. The chief of staff of the 24th Rifle Corps thanks a group of eight Il-2s for their actions outside Maslova Pristan." Also in a number of cases Soviet pilots reported that their attack aircraft had even been fired at by enemy tanks! "The fact that the target area was saturated with air defence artillery made it difficult for Il-2s to conduct counter-flak manoeuvres. It took at least twenty-to-

↻ Fitters prepare an Fw 190 for operations in the Belgorod sector.

thirty attack aircraft to suppress enemy air defence artillery" the 5th Guards ShAD headquarters reported.

Crisis

By 9 July the command of Army Group South had realised that it was unable to break through to Kursk along the Belgorod-Oboyan road, and decided to try to fight its way to the city from the south-east through the Psel River bend. According to German reconnaissance, the Soviet defences were not as strong there. However, the Supreme High Command General Headquarters redeployed various reserves to the area, and on the night of 10 July it renamed the Steppe Military District as the Steppe Front and ordered its commander General I.S. Konev to start deploying armies only at night. However, some of the armies had started their redeployment towards the enemy even before that, for example the 5th Guards Combined Arms Army and the 5th Guards Tank Army headed for Prokhorovka as early as July 7. In particular, tank units, headed by General P.A. Rotmistrov, were to cover in excess of 250 km, which was quite a difficult and unusual task, further complicated by the danger of *Luftwaffe* air strikes. This was probably the reason General Konev monitored the first stage of the march from an airborne U-2 aircraft.

As already mentioned, German aviation involved in Operation 'Zitadelle', was only strong enough to attack Soviet troops on the battlefield and in the immediate rear. Nevertheless, the *Luftwaffe* played an important part in frustrating the counter-attack of the 5th Guards Tank Army. However, it is worth mentioning that Soviet aircraft managed to fight their way through to enemy bombers and inflict losses on them several times. The most striking air engagement, involving eight Yak-1s and Yak-7bs from the 183rd IAP, took place on 11 July. Senior Lieutenant A.S. Yudin, tasked with protecting units of the 69th Army outside Belenikhino, detected a group of six Messerschmitts slightly below himself. He soon saw nine Ju 87s, escorted by six Bf 109s. Corps Commander General I.D. Podgorny ordered Yudin from the ground to let the Bf 109s pass and attack the Stukas head-on.

On seeing Soviet fighters approaching, the Messerschmitts started a combat turn, but lost sight of the Junkers in the clouds. The latter in their turn dropped their bombs in haste, and carried out an unfortunate manoeuvre, leaving their sides vulnerable to an attack from the Yaks. Yudin shot down one of the Ju 87s with his very first burst at a range of 100m after which he found himself amid German fighters. Junior Lieutenants Proskurin, Ovsyannikov, and Shemyakin rushed to rescue their leader. Several pilots managed to fire at individual Junkers at close range and as well as those pilots mentioned above, Junior Lieutenants Shishkin, Krasnov, and Agdantsev claimed air victories

↺ Loading a Pe-2.

⋂ Lieutenant N.G. Zavrazhin from the 427th IAP poses in front of the remains of a Bf 109 from JG52, which he had shot down on 27 July 1943.

⋂ Seen before a flight to Stalino are – from left to right: *Major* G.K. Höfer, II./KG55 *Gruppekommandeur*, *Oberst* E. Kühl *Geschwaderkommodore*, *Major* R. Ernst (Mayor of Strasburg, who during this battle, carried out a number of sorties as an observer in an He 111 bomber) and *Oberleutnant* R. Zeib, the *Staffelkapitän* of 6./KG55, seen at Kharkov Rogan airfield, 15 July 1943.

⋂ A Junkers Ju 87 Stuka.

⋂ A flight of La-5s from the 302nd IAD at Skorodnoye airfield.

as well. The latter shot down a Bf 109, and when recovering from the attack, he hit the rudder of a Junkers with his wing panel. The Junkers went into a spin and crashed to the ground outside the village of Bogoroditskoe. Six Bf 109s, probably tasked with 'clearing the airspace', dropped out of the sky to see no dive-bombers left in the area. Soviet pilots reported destroying two Messerschmitts and all nine Junkers aircraft. The German side admitted losing seven dive-bombers that day, with four Junkers destroyed in a single air engagement literally over the front line.

Other aircraft managed to break away under cover of their own air defence artillery, but the Luftwaffe lost five pilots from Squadron StG77, including the commander of 9./StG77 *Hauptmann* R. Bluemental. The Germans also confirmed a loss of a Messerschmitt from Group II./JG3, which caught fire and crashed into a

house in the village of Bogoroditskoe. Its pilot *Gefreiter* H. Schilling, who had just returned from hospital on 5 July, was killed in the crash. Again, despite the measures taken, Soviet aircraft failed to provide their own ground troops with reliable protection, and were unable to halt the enemy. General N.F. Vatutin decided to focus his major efforts on destroying units of the German 2nd SS Panzer Corps to seal the gap. The plan envisioned a powerful counter-attack against enemy tank divisions, with the ultimate objective of reaching Yakovlevo by the turn of the day. There seemed to be enough forces and assets: the 5th Guards Tank Army alone boasted in excess of 800 tanks and self-propelled guns, as well as up to 40,000 soldiers and officers. The 5th Guards Army, which had just arrived, as well as the 1st Tank Army and the 6th Guards Army, were to go on the offensive simultaneously in the south-eastern direction to joint with P.A. Rotmistrov's tank units, threatening to envelop German forces.

General Vatutin demanded that night bombers step up their activities. On the eve of the attack flight crews from the 262nd NBAD flew 164 sorties, aimed at bombing the rear of Army Group *Kempf* outside Razumnoe, Solomino, and Maslova Pristan, while the 208th NBAD carried out 109 sorties, targeting enemy troops and materiel north of Yakovlevo. P.S. Redchenkov, who was the first to take off, distinguished himself by destroying several searchlights, which allowed his comrades to operate in safer conditions. On the night of 12 July Redchenkov's U-2 biplane was seriously damaged by shrapnel, but the pilot managed to reach his home base and was decorated with the Order of the Red Star for his deed. Unlike ground units, the Voronezh Front aviation had not received any significant reinforcements since the outset of the Battle of Prokhorovka. Vatutin and Khrushchev asked Stalin to allocate two fighter air corps and an attack aircraft corps from the reserves of the Supreme High Command

General Headquarters in order to reinforce the 2nd Air Army as far back as July 8.

However, the Soviet commander-in-chief approved the transfer of just the 256th IAD, headed by Colonel N.S. Gerasimov, from the 8th SAK to the 2nd Air Army, commanded by Krasovskiy. The fully-equipped division operated ninety-six fighters, including forty-three brand new Yak-9s, the rest being the latest Yak-7bs. The strength of German air units decreased considerably as well and according to German sources, Group I./JG52, which had lost up to twenty Messerschmitts, nine pilots, and four mechanics, was withdrawn on July 12 and sent to Poltava to be reinforced. According to *Unteroffizier* A. Motsch, taken prisoner of war, his group I./SchG1 had lost twelve Fw 190s by that day as well. Group II./StG77 lost five flight crews, while Squadron KG27, which suffered fewer losses, sustained the greatest damage, one during a landing of a Heinkel on the Kharkov-Voytchenko airfield on July 5, and another during a bomber take-off from Poltava.

In addition to heavy losses, aviation activities were

A Pe-2 reconnaissance aircraft is prepared for a sortie from the Krasniy Kholm airfield. Here we see (from left to right) fitter Moiseenko, probationers Tsitrin and Vorovsky, and armament fitter Machnev.

A Ju 87G from 10.(Pz.)/StG2 is prepared for action.

Hauptman J. Menapace, *Staffelkapitän* of the 7./SG1 with his Henschel Hs 123 in July 1943. This unit often supported the forces of the *Heeresgruppe Kempf*.

An He 46C Biplane of 1.Nacht *Staffel, Luftflotte* 4.

◖ A Bf 109 from JG52 at Bessonovka airfield.

considerably interfered with by adverse weather conditions on July 12, especially in the morning. General S.A. Krasovskiy had to cancel take-offs of most attack aircraft squadrons until 10:00 hours, but later on Soviet aviation operated extremely intensively, making 759 combat sorties by nightfall. The enemy conducted only 654 sorties that day. Thus the 2nd Air Army surpassed the enemy in such an important index, of the number of combat sorties made, for the first time since the outbreak of the battle in the southern sector. The increase resulted primarily from the involvement of the 1st BAK, committed to combat once again after a long break. A total of about seventy flight crews had been waiting for a signal to take off since 03:30 hours, but the take-off had to be postponed until 07:45 hours due to low cloud cover. The most seasoned attack aircraft pilots took off at dawn and small Il-2 units delivered air strikes against the enemy at about 05:00 hours. At about the same time the 5th Guards Tank Army started closing in. Flight crews from the 1st ShAK attacked the enemy forward edge and it later transpired that they had attacked units of the 1st SS Panzer Division *Leibstandarte* SS Adolf Hitler. Groups were led by such experienced leaders as G.P. Aleksandrov, A.M. Glebov, B.V. Melnikov, M.P. Odintsov and M.I. Stepanov also attacked targets in the right flank rear of the 48th Tank Corps.

At the same time commanding officers of Soviet ground units repeatedly noted the active operations of enemy aviation, which "dominated over the battlefield." German aircraft from the 8th Air Corps started bombing combat formations of tank brigades who were preparing to launch attacks. The 5th Guards Tank Army headquarters started receiving an increasing number of reports about enemy bomb strikes against the advancing Soviet units at 10:00 hours. The headquarters of the 31st Tank Brigade, the 29th Tank Corps, reported: "Tanks suffered heavy losses to enemy air strikes and artillery fire. At 1030 hours tanks reached the village of Oktyabrskiy. Any further advance was

contained by non-stop enemy air strikes. Advancing tanks had had none of their own close air support until 13:00 hours. From 13:00 hours onwards close air support was provided by groups of two to ten fighters."

Almost every German combat sortie was now aimed at protecting the 2nd SS Panzer Corps or attacking the advancing Soviet troops. German Fw 190, Hs 123, and Hs 129 aircraft from the 8th Air Corps were all active over the front line on 12 July, attacking units of the 5th Guards Tank Army. The efficiency of their operations is shown in a report to the 5th Tank Army headquarters, which stated: "The enemy aviation wheeled over our combat formations, but there were not enough Soviet aircraft, especially fighters." The way the tank battle at Prokhorovka unfolded is well-known, and few readers will need to be convinced about the picture of a total defeat of 'Nazi tank hordes', painted by the Soviet history for years to come, which misrepresented the evidence – to put it mildly. In fact, the front-wide counter-attack failed to achieve its objectives, and although the tank crews fought heroically, most of them were killed in fierce battles.

The 5th Guards Tank Army had 189 of its tanks destroyed, and 140 more damaged, within a day and army Commander P.A. Rotmistrov also admitted the defeat in his memoirs. Attention should also be paid to one very important fact – the Soviet counter-attack targeted the enemy head-on, rather than at its flank. German reconnaissance aircraft, which had provided a timely warning of fresh Soviet corps being pulled up to the front line, had continued to watch the advancing tank units right until the outbreak of the battle. Soviet guardsmen later recalled that the enemy had zeroed-in its weapons at every critical point and set up ambushes, and prepared their anti-tank artillery guns for action. In other words, the enemy knew the exact location and strength of the counter-attack.

↻ Maria Mironenko, an exemplary armourer and member of the Young Communist League, prepares the warload for a Pe-2 bomber.

Chapter 4
Operation 'Zitadelle': The downfall

Both sides suffered enormous losses in the fierce battles outside Prokhorovka and the Soviet counter-attack of July 12 failed in its objectives, however Manstein's plan to defeat the 5th Guard Tank Army was frustrated as well. The flanks saw similar fierce battles and the Germans managed to drive back the 69th Army and almost overran A.S. Zhadov's guards. Meanwhile, the German forces were almost out of reserves and Manstein hoped that the *Führer* would allow the 5th SS Panzer Division 'Viking' and the entire 24th Panzer Corps to be thrown into action.

The aftermath of the Battle of Prokhorovka

When summoned to Hitler's headquarters on July 13 with *Generalfeldmarschall* von Kluge, Manstein gave the following figures in his report: Operation 'Zitadelle' had resulted in destroying 1,800 Soviet tanks, 267 field guns, and 1,080 anti-tank guns, as well as capturing 24,000 POWs. According to reports of the 8th Air Corps, a total of 524 Soviet aircraft were shot down in air engagements alone. The report produced a positive effect. After von Kluge's pessimistic

statement, the *Führer* seemed to have given up Operation 'Zitadelle', but Manstein convinced him that it was not over yet. He insisted that "after German forces had successfully repulsed attacks of the enemy, which had committed almost all of its operational reserves over the past few days, and the victory was close. To give up the battle now might mean missing out on victory!"

Manstein believed that if the German side stepped up the pressure, the Soviet command would be forced to give up its ongoing advance towards Orel and redeploy most of its combat-ready units to an area south of Kursk. However, such an upbeat assessment by the German was not globally agreed as most of his divisions had lost half of their tanks and assault guns (and an even greater percentage of armour), and, according to German documents, a total of 24,394 *Wehrmacht* soldiers and officers had been killed or injured. The 4th Air Fleet had a total of 200 of its aircraft destroyed or heavily damaged and in addition to the rising number of bomb strikes delivered by Allied aviation against many German cities, including Berlin; the German command was also worried about developments in Sicily and Italy. Thus, no aviation

↻ A gang of small boys beside a Fw 190 from JG54 which had been downed north of Kursk.

↻ Work taking place on an AM-38F engine from an Il-2 ground-attack aircraft.

↻ Work taking place on an AM-38F engine from an Il-2 ground-attack aircraft.

⋂ Soviet officers inspect the fragments of this dive bomber, shot down by anti-aircraft artillery. The fuselage markings suggest this was an aircraft of a unit leader.

units could be deployed from the west and the south-west to the east.

German reconnaissance provided information on the final preparations of the Red Army for an offensive in the Donetsk Basin and it was also clear that without powerful *Luftwaffe* air support the German side would not be able to repel, or at least halt, the Soviet advance towards either Stalino (Donetsk), or Orel. As a result, the German command arrived at a 'Scotch' verdict: Manstein should go on with the offensive, but without committing the 24th Panzer Corps, while portions of the air assets should be redeployed to the northern flank. Thus the commander of Army Group South was informed that his dive-bomber Groups I./StG2, III./StG2 and Fighter Group III./JG52 would be withdrawn from the 8th Air Corps by July 14.

Since I./JG52 had been withdrawn to the rear even earlier, the 8th Air Corps, especially its fighter and dive-bomber units, were weakened considerably although according to the German aces themselves, they were shooting down about twenty Soviet aircraft a day. Combat experience and an increased vigilance of Soviet flight crews, however, was now showing fewer losses as the activities of their aircraft and escort fighters became more coordinated as for instance,

⋂ Major P.I. Gavrilov, the CO of the 99th GvRAP, carried most of his 167 sorties in a Pe-2.

⋒ During the battle of Kursk, Junior Lieutenant A.E. Borovykh (later twice HSU) from the 157th IAP of the 273rd IAD, was credited with the destruction of six enemy aircraft flying a Yak-1 (serial number 14127).

documents of the 1st ShAK show that not a single Il-2 was lost to enemy fighters on 11–13 July (although quite a few flight crews were still reported missing in action). The *Luftwaffe's* final documents were still full of optimism and in a situation report on July 13 the 8th Air Corps headquarters said that just as before 'flight crews had provided most of their air support to advancing units of the 4th Panzer Army, while dive-bombers had destroyed targets in front of forward units of the 48th Panzer Corps and the 2nd SS Panzer Corps. German pilots claimed to have destroyed 25 Soviet tanks, and seven ammunition dumps, though results could only be observed in a few attacks due to a low cloud cover and adverse weather conditions.'

The documents also reported German losses and uncoordinated activities as well, for example, the 6th Panzer Army suffered heavy losses following an air strike, delivered by aircraft from the 291st ShAD, outside Kazachie and on the same day six Heinkels dropped their bombs 'precisely' on one of their own command posts, and this strike resulted in the deaths of five officers (including the commanding officer of the 144th Panzer Grenadier Regiment *Major* von Biberstein, and the battalion commander of the 6th Panzer Division Captain Jeckel, decorated with the Knight's Cross), fifteen *Unteroffiziers*, and the wounding of some fifty-six servicemen. The intensity

of battles did not slacken for three days after the Battle of Prokhorovka, and Manstein decided to capitalise on this and destroy units of the 69th Army, which had penetrated German positions. He ordered the 6th, the 19th Panzer, and the 168th Infantry Divisions, deployed outside Rzhavets, and the SS Panzer Division *Reich*, the SS Panzer Division *Adolf Hitler* and the 167th Infantry Division, which was deployed west of Prokhorovka, to deliver a simultaneous attack against Shakhovo, and to also encircle and destroy five divisions of the 48th Rifle Corps, with the 8th Air Corps providing close air support.

Once the realisation had dawned on the German command that Operation 'Zitadelle' had failed, the generals decided to exhaust Soviet troops as much as possible by conducting local operations. The German offensive continued at dawn on July 14 and its success was helped by improving weather allowing German aircraft to get airborne. It turned out later on that VNOS posts registered a total of 3,274 enemy combat sorties throughout the entire Soviet-German front that day and German aviation reported over 4,677 combat sorties. No doubt the *Luftwaffe* did not intend to give up its air superiority in the Battle of Kursk, and according to German documents, units of the 6th Air Fleet and the 8th Air Corps conducted 2,431 combat sorties, with the latter making 1,452 sorties by sunset.

General H. Seidemann must have decided to crush as many Soviet positions as possible and thus threw everything available in one last push, capitalising no doubt on the favourable weather and knowing that about 120 aircraft were to be redeployed to the northern flank.

According to German sources, Ju 87 Stukas encountered a large number of attacks from both Soviet fighters and heavy flak on the approaches to Prokhorovka, but only lost three Junkers (rather than the seventeen Ju 87s reported by pilots from the 256th IAD). The aircraft, piloted by the commander of 8./StG77 *Hauptman* H. Werner, blew up in mid air after a direct hit by an AA round, and another commanding officer, *Oberleutnant* G. Schmidt (who had been decorated with the Knight's Cross and had

made in excess of 700 combat sorties) was shot down by Soviet fighters – the latter may have been shot down by navigator A.S. Romanenko from the 91st IAP. Commanding officer of III./JG3 *Major* W. Ewald was also shot down over German positions outside Shakhovo, at around 15:00 hours and according to German sources, the ace, who had scored seventy-seven victories, was hit by friendly fire.

Manstein, who was enjoying *Luftwaffe* close air support also managed to capture the village of Shakhovo and encircle three divisions of the Soviet 48th Rifle Corps. Several Soviet units had managed to fight their way through to the main forces at night, but suffered heavy losses. However Soviet troops still held their ground in other parts of the front as German historian W. Gerliz later commented: "On July 10–15,

◑ An Illyushin long-range bomber lands after a sortie.

◑ A recovery crane handles this Fw 190A from JG51 after a landing 'mishap'.

◑ The flak mounting on the APC, destroyed by a Soviet ground-attack aircraft.

↻ Maria Sergeeva, preparing the ammunition for ground-attack aircraft.

♠ Senior Lieutenant N.I. Semyontsov (left) and Captain
N.T. Kitaev from 8th GvIAD were both successful Soviet
fighter pilots in the Kursk battle.

♠ A Fieseler Fi 156C ambulance aircraft taking off.

1943 Manstein and his advancing units managed to reach the watershed between Donets, Psel, Seym, and Vorksla, but were by now both exhausted and depleted". The offensive halted at the Shebekino hills, in the woods near a village of Gonki, next to the Belgorod-Oboyan road. Later on General Konev mentioned the 'swan song' of German armour: "The last combat-ready panzer units were burning on the battlefield, and turning into ashes..."

The Germans go on the defensive

The German command decided to retreat to the starting point of its summer offensive and thus approximately twelve aviation groups were withdrawn from the 8th Air Corps and redeployed to other locations. On July 15 the 8th Air Corps made some 706 combat sorties, and on July 17 combat missions were flown by only 138 aircraft, with a considerable number of them sporting Hungarian identification marks. By the same token the 2nd Air Army made 328 and 484 combat sorties respectively. Thus, the situation in the air changed to the advantage of the Red Army Air Force, and the enemy were forced out as Soviet aviation dominated the sky. In order to avoid any further heavy losses the Germans rearranged their air defence artillery and reinforced convoy protection in certain areas. Soviet flight crews now operated with a greater intensity even at night, and suffice to say that U-2s from the 208th NBAD undertook the lion's share of missions during the evenings of July 12–18 making some 1,169 combat sorties, which amounted to 2.95 sorties per night per each operational U-2. Pilots repeatedly received letters of commendation from their own troops and the Soviet archives store a telegram from the 1st Tank Army headquarters to General Krasovsky: "Today on 18 July I spent the day with General Getman's advance units and saw a group of nine Il-2s attack an enemy motor convoy of about 200–250 vehicles with trailers on the Dubrava-Butovo road at 15:15 hours. Commanding officers and I were simply delighted with the results of the attack. Escort fighters operated well. There were no enemy aircraft in the sky". The Soviet command now focused its efforts on liberating Belgorod and Kharkov. However, Soviet units, exhausted by the fierce battles, were too tired to go on with the offensive and Zhukov persuaded Stalin to give the troops a break to regroup. Offensive Operation 'Polkovodets Rumyantsev' was now high on the agenda.

The battle on the southern sector of the Orel-Kursk area turned out to be even fiercer and bloodier than the one on the northern sector, and the German offensive on the southern sector lasted even longer – as even on July 11 Manstein still hoped to breach 'the last Soviet defensive line' and fight his way through to Kursk from the south. However unfolding events saw the commander of Army Group South completely give up Operation "Zitadelle' and start retreating. The German command was still quite upbeat about the situation north of Belgorod for quite a long time and had managed to repel several counter-attacks mounted by the Voronezh Front, with the most powerful one launched outside Prokhorovka on July 12. Although during each clash the Germans suffered fewer losses than the Soviets, the intensive battles over such a wide front gradually exhausted the German strike force. The Germans realised that the Soviet offensive, mounted against the 2nd Panzer Army on July 12, was aimed at defeating their entire force outside Orel, and Hitler, who was also concerned about developments in Sicily, was resigned to the situation and was "forced to tell the commanding officers of both army groups, taking part in Operation 'Zitadelle' to give up the

○ Soviet armoured trains carrying heavy AA played a vital role in defending the Soviet land forces.

○ Major P.A. Pologov, CO of the 163rd IAP, clambers out from his Yak-9.

⊃ View of Prokhorovka battlefield. Taken after the fighting from a U-2 aircraft.

operation on July 13."

Manstein stated: "After Operation 'Zitadelle' had failed, the Soviet side completely seized the initiative in the eastern theatre of operations. After we had failed to encircle large enemy forces in the area of the Kursk area… the numerical superiority inevitably started having its effect. The enemy offensive in the Orel-Kursk area was just the beginning of the all-out strategic offensive of the Red Army." Massive heroism and improving proficiency and skills of Red Army soldiers and officers, as well as the fact that they were now equipped with cutting-edge and modern weapons, allowed Soviet troops to halt the enemy. The Soviet Air Force was not passive at the outbreak of the battle on the southern sector of the Kursk area; on the contrary, Soviet air strikes, delivered against German airfields outside Belgorod and Kharkov in the small hours of July 5 were aimed at tipping the balance of forces sharply in favour of the Soviet side. Under the plan developed by Soviet military leaders the decisive suppression of the enemy and inflicting significant losses would make the task of establishing air superiority considerably easier.

Soviet sources admit that they did not manage to establish air superiority in the course of fierce air engagements of the first few days, but they insist that the objective was fulfilled in the Belgorod region by July 11. However, analysis of both the Soviet and German archives and the number of enemy combat sorties made do not give grounds for such a conclusion. At the most crucial moments in the campaign the *Luftwaffe* focused its efforts on the main axis of advance and inflicted heavy losses on Soviet ground troops and materiel, and the Red Army Air Force managed to establish air superiority only after the 4th Panzer Army and Army Group *Kempf* had ended their active combat operations, and most units of the 8th Air Corps had been redeployed to other locations, and their fierce air engagements resulted in tremendous losses. According to a report from the 2nd Air Army headquarters, a total of 371 aircraft were lost from 5 to the 18 July, and should the losses of the 17th Air Army (at least 200 aircraft) be taken into account? One may conclude that about 600 Soviet aircraft were destroyed in battles outside Belgorod and Kharkov, however, the enemy also lost about half its aircraft.

⋔ Crews of the 81st GvBAP novice crews during practice flights.

⋃ Junior Lieutenant V.P. Aleksukhin from the 617th ShAP in front of an Il-2 with the 'Alexander Suvorov' logo and the 'Suvorov Order' on the tailfin.

◗ *Luftwaffe* groundcrew marked the successes of their aircraft against Soviet armour, and here we see the tailfin of an Hs 129B flown by *Oberleutnant* P.H. Ruffer and his tally of thirteen destroyed tanks. According to *Luftwaffe* records, before his death in July 1944 his score rose to eighty!

◗ *General* H. Hoth, the Commander of 4. *Panzerarmee* reviewing front-line positions.

↻ Captain B.F. Shubin, the squadron CO from the 800th ShAP was killed in action on 14 July 1943.

↻ During the Belgorod defensive operation, Captain M.S. Malov, the squadron CO from 800th ShAP led his ground-attack aircraft in some fourteen missions.

★ ✠ **Table 5: Losses in the Kursk area of operations**

Losses *	German losses		Soviet losses
	Irreplaceable	Repairable	Irreplaceable
Northern face	110-120	70-80	391
Southern face	240	up to 200	371 + over 200
Total	**350-360**	**270-280**	**Over 1,000**

* On the northern sector Luftwaffe losses were registered from 5 until 11 July, and Red Army Air Force losses were registered from 5 until 12 July, and on the southern sector losses of both sides were registered from 5 until 18 July.

Note: The column of total Soviet losses takes into account aircraft in service with the Long-Range Aviation and the Air Defence Forces, as well as the 2nd Air Army, destroyed in the battle area from 19 until 23 July. As is clear from the table, the German side lost considerably more than 193 aircraft on both sectors of the battle from 5 until 15 July, contrary to the claims of most western sources. Western sources based their calculations on interim reports given in combat operations logbooks, while the author has used the reports of the Luftwaffe Quartermaster General, considered to be significantly more comprehensive.

⋔ The intensive flying during the battle demanded exhaustive work by the fitters and mechanics. Here a DB 605A engine is inspected near Belgorod.

⋔ Repairing the combat damage to a Bf 109G.

⋔ Squadron pilots and members of the 'Young Communist League' discuss recent operations beside a Yak-7B fighter.

⋔ A Junkers Ju 88D from 4(F)./121 with a damaged tail, inflicted by Soviet AA artillery at Seshcha airfield.

According to rough calculations, the 8th Air Corps suffered about 170 'combat losses' (as defined by the Germans) and about seventy 'non-combat losses during combat operations', while up to 200 aircraft were heavily damaged in the same period. Based on documents from both sides, total losses suffered in the course of defensive operations outside Kursk, can be thus assessed and the data is given in Table 5 (page 72).

It seems that the ratio of irreplaceable losses of 1 to 2:8 reflected an average level of skill and combat experience, as well as survivability of aircraft. A total of nine pilots, decorated with the 'Knight's Cross', were either killed in action or taken POW and it was extremely difficult to find fully-fledged replacements for them. Subordinates of General S.A. Krasovsky were more successful in countering German aviation than their comrades-in-arms from the 16th Air Army. Pilots from the 5th IAK, with some of the greatest Soviet aces, achieved impressive results in the course of battle, although the word 'ace' was not used widely in Soviet documents in summer 1943. However, corps and divisional commanding officers emphasised that only a small percentage of flight crews destroyed enemy aircraft in dogfights on a regular basis.

Commander of the 5th IAK, General D.P. Galunov stated: "A relatively small number of pilots regularly shoot down several enemy aircraft. For instance, only 37 pilots of the corps (who scored five or more victories) shot down 183 aircraft, which amounted to 40% of all aircraft shot down in the course of the Belgorod operation." Attack aircraft probably played an even greater role in the Belgorod direction than in the north as Il-2s made up to 360 combat sorties a day and inflicted huge losses on the enemy. The 2nd Air Army headquarters stated: "The efficiency of bomb strikes, delivered by the 291st ShAD, is also considerably higher than that of other units. Virtues of this division include better organisation and preparation for combat sorties, and a higher combat training of flight crews, and credit should also be given to the pilots of the 737th IAP, who escorted attack aircraft and fought as part of the 291st ShAD".

Chapter 5

Operation 'Kutuzov': The counter offensive

When planning the counter-offensive in Orel, the Soviet High Command's goal was to smash the troops of the 9th Field and 2nd Tank Armies, and to create the conditions for a general offensive by the Red Army to the West. To realise these plans, it was suggested that powerful strikes be made by the armies on the Western, Bryansk and Central Fronts to encircle the enemy's forces, split them and annihilate their constituent parts. The units on the left flank of the Western Front (under the command of Colonel-General V.D. Sokolovsky) were tasked to break through the enemy's defences and together with the right-flank army on the Bryansk Front, they were to destroy the German forces near Bolkhov. The troops of the Bryansk Front, headed by Colonel-General M.M. Popov, were to make two strikes, one in the direction of Bolkhov, join the Western Front, and then make a second strike from Novosil to Orel in order to surround the enemy's forces. The troops of the Central Front, under the command of Army General Rokossovsky, were to move to Orel from the south and the offensive would be supported by the 1st Air Army of General M.M. Gromov, the 15th Air Army of General N.F. Naumenko, and the 16th Air Army of General S.I. Rudenko.

Thus the following tasks were also set for the Soviet aviation regiments:

- To hold supremacy in the air and provide reliable top cover for the offensive forces
- To assist ground troops in breaching the enemy's defence
- To prevent the enemy's forces from getting into defensive positions at the rear,
- To hinder the enemy forces' command efforts and to disturb the manoeuvring of any reserves in order to prevent their approach to the front line.

Personnel of the 30th GvIAP in front of a P-39 fighter.

⋂ Yak-9 fighter – its performance was not inferior to the newest Bf 109G-6.

↻ Armament technician V. Shumkova prepares the bomb load of a Pe-2 for its next sortie.

⋂ Lieutenant General N.F. Naumenko, commander of the 15th Air Army.

↻ Production of two-seat Il-2s at Factories No.1 and 18 at Kuybishev increased considerably in spring 1943.

The headquarters of the High Command also tasked Soviet Long-Range Aviation with supporting the front-line aviation units with powerful nocturnal raids. The plans for combat activities of the 1st, 15th and 16th Air Armies were quickly developed on the first day of the counter-offensive and it was expected that any further actions would depend on the situation at the front. The main efforts in the air were to be concentrated towards strikes against ground forces, and air superiority was intended to be reached by destroying the enemy in the air. Specially allocated fighter units would provide air support to the offensive forces of the fronts and before starting any ground attack, the aircraft of the 1st and 15th Air Armies would be tasked with building up a smoke screen. Plans of the forthcoming combat had certain specifics. For example, the 15th Air Army would have to support two areas on the ground, while the 16th Air Army would concentrate its main attacks on the ground troops. Special attention was given for the continuity of air support, and the Soviet command emphasised the need for reliable cooperation with those on the ground. Unlike the defensive operation, the number of aviation command posts equipped with up-to-date communication and their positioning was crucial, especially in the battle areas. They also established primary air control posts, and the extensive network of radio stations was improved in order to direct Soviet aircraft to the enemy targets.

On the eve of the offensive, air reconnaissance was given a primary importance, and a number ground posts were deployed into the combat zones. These

⋔ Ju 88 of III./KG1 in flight.

posts were equipped for supporting day and night flights, and used different communication methods including radio beacons, campfires, searchlights and smoke signals. Before starting the counter-offensive, the High Command further increased the number of combat units at the front, as for example, the 1st Air Army received from the reserves the 8th IAK commanded by General F.F. Zherebchenko, the 2nd ShAK of General V.V. Stepichev, the 2nd BAK of General V.A. Ushakov, as well as several other separate units. As a result, taking into account the 2nd IAK of General A.S. Blagoveschensky which was added to the Army's strength in May, the Air Army now included fourteen air divisions with fifty-seven regiments. Along with the Yaks, Il's, Pe's, and La's which were widely used on all fronts, the army now had Hurricanes of the 179th Separate Fighter Air Regiment, an air observation squadron using the Su-2 plus, new Yak-9T's (with 37mm cannon) and Yak-9Ds (with the increased fuselage fuel tanks) were combat tested at the 18th GvIAP of the 303rd IAD. As most of the units of the 1st and 15th Air Armies didn't participate in the battle for Kursk, they were able to prepare themselves for the coming offensive. Second-line units also had enough capacity for eight to ten days operations, and also teams were established to clear mines from airfields left by the retreating enemy forces.

The primary goal – the capture of Bolkhov

The Bolkhov operation at Bryansk and the Western Fronts, which started at dawn on July 12, became one of the decisive operations in the Orlov area. The counter-offensive by the Soviet army started following powerful artillery and air strikes, and at the breakthrough area forces of the 2nd BAK, 2ShAK, as well as the 224th and 223rd ShAD were in attendance, and on the eve of the operation night bomber units (Long-Range Aviation and 213th NBAD) carried out strikes. At the Bryansk Front preliminary air strikes were undertaken, however night bombing from light aviation exhausted the enemy troops on the evening before the operation. In the morning ground troops began their counter-offensive cutting into the enemy's defences in some areas as far as 25 km, and were supported by a smoke screen cover previously set up by the attack aircraft. Assisting the troops of General V.D. Sokolovsky, some seventy Soviet aircraft made continuous strikes on the enemy's artillery positions and strong points, and attack aircraft pounded the enemy trenches, shelters and artillery positions whilst the fighter units patrolled above.

During the first day the Soviet the troops on the Western Front, with the support of the units of the 1st Air Army, breached the enemy's defences, surmounting the first and second German defence lines and establishing conditions for motorised units to enter the battle. On the first day of the battle, some 240 tons of bombs were dropped on the German positions and crews reported that they had destroyed some twenty-one enemy tanks, fifty-five trucks, and twelve artillery batteries. The offensive at the Bryansk Front was far more difficult, and by the late morning of the operation, German aviation had considerably increased its activity towards the main Soviet armies, and from July 12, the groups of attacking German bombers increased from eight to ten aircraft, to over thirty bombers and dive bombers, with up to twenty fighters also on station.

According to German sources, units of the 6th Air Fleet carried out 1,111 sorties on July 12, mostly over the Bryansk Front where fighters shot down eighty-seven Soviet aircraft for the loss of just thirteen. German records confirm victories by Major A.M. Chislov of the 63rd GvIAP, Senior Lieutenant P.I. Muravyov of the 64th GvIAP and others. But undoubtedly, Soviet aviation failed to attain air superiority in this area, and experienced heavy losses, with the most serious impact being felt by the 225th ShAD and the 1st GvIAK. General E.M. Beletsky later recalled: "The main task for the Corps was to fight for air superiority over the breakthrough area. The fighter support was usually not allocated to secondary tasks, and all forces were concentrated to the main battle area. Such an approach proved itself, and the Corps found

favourable conditions that allowed them to make powerful strikes on the enemy's aviation in the air".

While the airfields of the Soviet fighter units worked like a conveyor belt, releasing the units one after the other according to their schedule, small groups of fighters were quickly scattered and easily destroyed by the superior forces of the *Luftwaffe*, and many German aces were able to increase their combat scores, and the Commanders of I./JG51 *Major* E. Leie and 12./JG51 *Hauptmann* W. Moritz, and a pilot of II./JG54 *Leutnant* G. Scheel, each scored five victories. According to reports from the 1st GvIAK, during two days of combat they lost over twenty-nine pilots and forty-five aircraft, and it was not only the novices who lost their lives, but experienced Soviet aces as well. Amongst this number was the 64th GvIAP's Lieutenant N.M. Alekseev, who by that time had been presented with the Gold Star as a Hero of the Soviet Union (HSU), and the Squadron Commander of the 32nd GvIAP, HSU Captain A.F. Moshin,

On the afternoon of July 12 some eighty-nine Il-4 bombers of the 113th BAD were engaged in actions at

◖ An attack aircraft of the 78th GvShAP is being prepared for combat. Pilot Junior Lieutenant Zhdanov is in the cockpit, while the gunner/radio operator Sergeant Lyashchenko stays on the wing.

◖ Technicians of I./JG51 prepare an Fw 190A for another sortie.

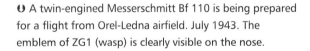

◗ A twin-engined Messerschmitt Bf 110 is being prepared for a flight from Orel-Ledna airfield. July 1943. The emblem of ZG1 (wasp) is clearly visible on the nose.

◖ German pilots congratulate *Staffelkapitän* of 1./JG51 *Oberleutnant* J. Brendel, after shooting down his 50th enemy aircraft. Orel-Sloboda airfield.

the Bryansk Front, and dropped more than 500 HE and 3,000 fragmentation bombs on enemy positions. Small groups of twin-engined Me 110s had made several attacks on these groups of Ilyushin bombers over the front line, but failed make an impact. The crews of the Soviet long-range bombers had a notion that the idea of using the Il-4s as front-line bombers came from the Supreme Commander-in-Chief, as during one of the conferences in spring 1943, Stalin expressed wanting to use the Il-4 units not only at night, but also during the day with fighter support. The 113th BAD had been in reserve for several months and on the eve of the Soviet offensive they were transferred to the command of General N.F. Naumenko in order to assist in breaking through the enemy's defences. On the first day of the battle the losses were small (two bombers were shot down, and two others collided in the air), but on the second day, due to poor in-flight manoeuvring, the battle formations were more lax, allowing fighters from III./JG51 to set six bombers on fire whilst losing only one of its own (*Unteroffizier* F. Meindl was shot down after destroying four Il-4 bombers). In total twelve of the thirty-six bombers did not return home and the crews noted as 'unacceptable' the fighter cover provided by the 4th GvIAD. In their opinion the 'inactivity' of the fighter pilots, and poor coordination between the crews of different units, were the main reasons for their heavy losses.

On 13 July, in the same way as the 113th BAD, the 225th ShAD also experienced heavy losses with some thirty Illyushin bombers being shot down (i.e. the whole regiment), but some of these aircraft were later found to have made emergency landings and were eventually repaired. One of the reasons given for the losses was the command's attempt to introduce a 'free hunting' method for the poorly trained crews. For example, in the 783th ShAP, the main crews were senior lieutenants and recent graduates of the flight schools, but had not completed any specialised combat training. As a result these 'hunters', flying in pairs, turned into 'fair-game' for the German fighters. Even six-aircraft formations of Il-2s hardly defended themselves from the enemy's attacks without losses as the Soviet pilots were unable to get into a 'defensive circle' formation in time, so the last aircraft to break formation were quickly lost. The crews of the 225th ShAD and 3rd ShAK complained bitterly about the fighter cover, which was poorly arranged. For example, a group of the 624th ShAK, with some forty-two attack aircraft, was covered by only three Yak fighters of the 66th GvIAP, and German Focke-Wulfs were able to pick off the Soviet aircraft, claiming amongst others the unit commander, Major Vyalov.

The air combat which took place above the tank positions commanded by General M.F. Panov could be considered as typical for such battles. An eight-aircraft formation of La-5s of the 32nd GvIAP of the 1st GvIAK, lead by Captain V.I. Garanin, was carrying out an air patrol over the area and attacked a pair of Ju 88s, which managed to escape, then a group of Ju 87s covered by Fw 190s was seen as was a single Fw 189 spotter plane. However despite the whole unit engaging this solitary aircraft they failed to shoot it down and were pounced on by the German fighters. Because the Soviet fighters had been drawn away, the German dive bombers dropped their payload on the tank corps. The combat actions record book of the 6th Air Fleet state that as the result of air strikes, thirty-two Russian tanks were destroyed and a further twenty-five damaged. Around this time and because of

❂ One of the pilots of I./JG54 taking off for a mission in the Orel area.

○ Technicians and armourers prepare the aircraft of *Hauptmann* M. Franzisket at Orel-Ledna airfield. According to German records, this pilot died on 19 July, when commanding I./ZG1, after an anti-aircraft shell hit his Bf 110G.

○ Commander of the 6th Air Fleet *Generaloberst* Robert Ritter von Greim (second from right) with a group of headquarters officers in the vicinity of Smolensk.

○ General-inspector of fighter aviation of the Eastern Front H. Trautloft at a parade of the personnel of *Jagdgeschwader Mölders*.

○ He 111 bombers of one of the groups of KG53 Legion Condor in combat formation.

a mistake by Soviet command personnel, a four-aircraft formation of Il-2s of the 198th ShAP, 233rd ShAD, led by the Squadron Commander Captain V.A. Malinkin, took off without air cover and was immediately spotted by German Me 110s. Three Il-2s were lost in fierce fighting, and only the aircraft of Lieutenant A.N. Efimov (at that time a little-known pilot, but later on Marshal of Aviation, twice HSU) successfully returned to home base and reported shooting down a two-engined Messerschmitt.

Already when planning the Operation 'Zitadelle', the German Command considered the possibility of Soviet counter-strike on the flank of the 9th Army. In order to prevent this threat *Generaloberst* W. Model, who had under his command the troops of the 8th Field and 2nd Tank Armies, began urgently moving his

forces into that area, thus in a short space of time up to ten formations, including tanks, entered the battle and turned the balance in favour of the Germans. In addition, the main effort of German bombers and dive bombers was concentrated in this area, and with Soviet fighters providing continuous air cover to the offensive ground formations fierce air engagements took place.

The height of the air battle over the Western Front was on July 14, when the Germans directed their efforts in this area. The command of the 1st Air Army was ready for such events and General M.M. Gromov repeatedly warned his subordinates about complacency. The units of the 6th Air Fleet carried out 979 sorties, with about two-thirds of them strike missions, and air observation posts reported over 600 German aircraft (300 He 111, Ju 88 and Bf 110 bombers

♦ *Sturmpanzer* IV *Brummbär* self-propelled gun destroyed by Soviet aviation.

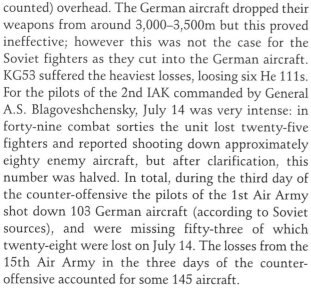

♦ Remains of a shot-down Junkers.

♦ Soviet artillerymen prepare to open fire. In the course of the battle, the anti-aircraft battery of Lieutenant Barybin shot down four German aircraft.

counted) overhead. The German aircraft dropped their weapons from around 3,000–3,500m but this proved ineffective; however this was not the case for the Soviet fighters as they cut into the German aircraft. KG53 suffered the heaviest losses, loosing six He 111s. For the pilots of the 2nd IAK commanded by General A.S. Blagoveshchensky, July 14 was very intense: in forty-nine combat sorties the unit lost twenty-five fighters and reported shooting down approximately eighty enemy aircraft, but after clarification, this number was halved. In total, during the third day of the counter-offensive the pilots of the 1st Air Army shot down 103 German aircraft (according to Soviet sources), and were missing fifty-three of which twenty-eight were lost on July 14. The losses from the 15th Air Army in the three days of the counter-offensive accounted for some 145 aircraft.

The Germans also paid a heavy price as according to Luftwaffe records the losses of the 6th Air Fleet were increasing day by day, and they had lost up to sixteen aircraft on July 12, twenty the next day, and twenty-four on 14 July. For the Germans, July 13 saw the fiercest and bloodiest battles, as JG51 lost eight Fw 190s, with four pilots missing (including *Oberleutnant* A. Walter who had scored thirty-five victories), one pilot became a POW and two were

wounded. On the same day *Kommodore* ZG1 *Ritterkreuzträger Major* J. Blechshmidt was shot down and taken prisoner together with his air gunner. On the next day the Group I./ZG1 lost its commander, *Hauptmann* W. Herrmann, shot down by anti-aircraft artillery. Also on July 14 three Bf 110s of *Panzerjagdstaffel* Pz./ZG1 were shot down and the same number of aircraft was damaged, and by the end of the day only one serviceable aircraft remained with the unit.

The Orel Operation

On July 13 1943 Mussolini contacted Hitler with a request to strengthen the aviation forces in Italy by taking units from the Eastern Front, to provide support for troops fighting in Sicily. Il Duce stated in his telegram that 'the moral and military consequences of the enemy's defeat (i.e. British and American forces – author) after its first attempt in a European offensive will be huge'. Hitler ordered Göring to send no less than eight air groups from south-eastern Europe, France and Germany, but nothing from the Soviet-German front. However, the German command had few reserves for the 6th Air Fleet, which was already carrying out intensive air combat in the East. At the time of the Soviet counter-offensive, the Fleet had slightly more than forty serviceable fighters, so the Germans urgently relocated the 12./JG54 to the Orel region. *Generaloberst* H. Jeschonnek also ordered the 1st Air Division of the 6th Air Fleet to be strengthened by III./JG52, *Stab* I./StG2, III./StG2, II./KG27, and several anti-tank and attack units. This allowed the Germans to almost double the number of air sorties, compared to those carried out in the first days of the Soviet counter-offensive. The Soviet command replenished their losses mostly by single crews, which were arriving from the reserve regiments. However, after three days of battle many of the units were seriously weakened, especially with of serviceable aircraft. For example, the 3rd GvIAD lost more than half of their La-5s and La-5FNs, while by July 15 the 4th GvIAD had only a small number of serviceable Yaks (64th GvIAP, 9; 65th GvIAP, 16; and 66th GvIAP, 8). The 234th IAD, which was returned from the Central

Front, became a significant help.

It was also decided to use this Division in fighting on the Bryansk Front. The pilots of the Corps thus carried out air patrols over the Soviet troops and escorted bombers and attack aircraft. For example, in the morning of 15 July a group of Il-2s of the 893rd ShAP took off for a combat mission covered by Yaks from the 65th GvIAP. One air engagement was especially dramatic when a group of attack aircraft, led by Lieutenant Colonel Khromov and making his third sortie of the day, were on patrol when a four-aircraft formation of Focke-Wulfs suddenly emerged from the clouds and headed for the Soviet attack aircraft. The leading Fw 190 aimed at the aircraft flown by Khromov. The Soviet fighter did not have time to react, so Junior Lieutenant P.E. Korolev, who was the nearest to the attacking enemy, immediately turned his Yak-1 in for a head-on attack against the leading Fw 190. The

◔ Captain A.S. Sibirin after a successful sortie in his Yak-9. On 14 July 1943 he shot down an Fw 190, which became the fifth victory of the 18th GvIAP's squadron commander.

◑ Inspection of an Fw 190 between sorties.

◔ Boston bomber being prepared for a combat sortie. The gunner is already at his position, while the other crew members clarifiy the mission plan.

◑ Il-2 attack aircraft often returned to their home base with such damage.

∩ An anti-aircraft artillery gunner reviews the cockpit of an Airacobra belonging to the 30th GvIAP.

aircraft collided and both pilots perished. Most likely, the victim of this ram attack was the German ace, *Leutnant* G. Scheel of I./JG54.

The units of the 1st and 15th Air Armies carried out bombing and ground attack strikes on the enemy's forces to the west and south of the breakthrough area, and their main efforts were concentrated on supporting the 1st and 25th Tank Corps. Also columns of the German tanks and armoured vehicles were moving up from the rear and from other directions, and were almost parallel to the front line, but were not attacked. However, when entering the battle, they were targeted by Il-2s and Pe-2s. In the meanwhile, the Soviet command also brought new forces into the battle for Orel. The Central Front started the counter-offensive on July 15, and aviation activity increase considerably. On the previous day, Commander of the 16th Air Army General S.I. Rudenko noted in his combat log that the Germans were forced to move their air force units to other areas, thus allowing for a swift spurt by the Soviet troops.

The plan of action, developed by army headquarters, also included a massive, four-wave air strike by the 16th Air Army. In fact, the Soviet aviation units made three concentrated strikes, each by a group

of up 300 aircraft. In total, on July 15 the 16th Air Army carried out 1,002 sorties, while the enemy responded with only forty flights. The overwhelming amount of munitions dropped allowed the Soviet army quickly to overrun the German positions. On the following day, *Luftwaffe* activities increased noticeably, and the German ground troops made numerous counter-attacks. However, Soviet aviation made another three massive strikes, with three-hour intervals, on the German 9th Army. Each of the strikes involved more than 400 aircraft. The first group consisted of 410 aircraft (155 bombers, 101 attack aircraft, and 154 fighters), the second – 444 planes (140 bombers, 123 attack aircraft, and 181 fighters), while the third group was the most numerous – 460 planes (146 bombers, 126 attack aircraft, and 188 fighters). In total, Soviet aviation made some 1,713 sorties.

Undoubtedly the German air defence forces could not provide reliable cover for their troops; however, reports from that period do record successes. An information bulletin from the German intelligence department dated July 16 spoke of the destruction of 949 Soviet aircraft by German fighters from 1 – 15 July, while a further seventy-two aircraft were shot down by artillery. The combat log of the 6th Air Fleet for the same day shows 1,776 sorties (both combat and transport), and 968.34 tons of bombs and 1,444 leaflets dropped. The next day, JG54 celebrated the 5,000th enemy aircraft shot down since the beginning of the war and the records also show that II./KG53 made its 10,000th sortie and the KG4 its 30,000th! Other losses noted were that of a Junkers, flown by the Commander of 1./StG1 *Hauptmann* F. Lorenz being hit an artillery shell at low altitude when exiting a dive, while the Commander of 2./StG2 *Hauptmann* E. Jaekel was killed in air combat with the fighters of the 234th IAD. Most likely he was hit by pilot Radchenko, ex-commander of the 248th IAP, who was reduced to the ranks because of a disciplinary case.

On July 17 one of the most experienced anti-tank pilots Commander of 4(Pz.)/SchG2 *Oberleutnant* B. Meyer was also very close to being killed, as according to his recollections, the Russians piloted their Yak-9 fighters excellently, and knew the weak points of the Hs 129 and fired accurately. Meyer released the canopy and bailed out, but his canopy was caught by the air flow and flew straight into the engine of a Yak and the fighter caught fire. The Soviet pilot made an emergency landing, and after hitting the ground Meyer ran to the Soviet plane and was amazed when he found a dead female pilot in the cockpit of the fighter. According to Soviet documents she was Junior Lieutenant A.V. Lebedeva of the 65th GvIAP.

The 16th Air Army was under maximum stress during the first three days of counter-offensive, and the subordinates of General S.I. Rudenko carried out 4,458 sorties and reported twenty-eight aircraft shot down in twenty-two air engagements for the loss of fifty-two aircraft. Summarizing the results of massive air raids from the 16th Air Amy, Deputy Commander of the Red Army Air Force, General-Colonel F.A. Falaleev noted that the Soviet losses in case of massive air

strikes were about three times lower than when attacking in small groups. Moreover, he emphasized a considerable moral impact on the enemy: "In order to mislead the enemy about the quantity of attacking aircraft and number of sorties, the bombers dropped only half of the bomb load in the first strike. Then the aircraft flew back to their own territory and then returned to drop their remaining bombs.

This action created the impression that the enemy had more aircraft than they actually did". It should be mentioned that both German and Soviet allies participated air combat over the Western front. Among the German number was a Spanish fighter unit 15(span.)/JG51 headed by Major Mariano Cuadra, and French volunteer pilots fought in the 'Normandie' squadron of the 303rd IAD, flying Yak-1 and Yak-9 fighters for the Soviets. By the evening of July 17, the French squadron had scored thirty victories (eighteen of them during the counter-offensive by the Red Army), while the unit had lost fifteen aircraft and ten pilots, with the heaviest losses inflicted during the latter days.

The German ground troops now fought much harder, and often counter-attacked – 'While the armies allocated from the reserves were strengthening the Bryansk and Western Fronts, the enemy quickly relocated the divisions of the 9th Army from other positions in order to counteract our troops' – noted the head of the Bryansk Front, General L.M. Sandalov. 'It should be noted that our aviation could not slow down the approach of German reserves to the battlefield. Due to this, the superiority of our forces at the breakthrough areas was decreasing day after day. During the next three days, 15–17 July, the offensive on the Bryansk Front slowed down further'. The German counteraction in the air noticeably increased where the Soviet command had introduced tank units

◑ German pilots discuss a combat mission. In the centre – *Hauptmann* G.G. Marufka from 4./SchG2

◑ A German artillery tractor with 37mm anti-aircraft cannon escorting a truck column.

⋂ A new type of German aircraft – the anti-tank Ju 87G.

⋂ A group of Pe-2 bombers in combat.

or groups. Already on July 14 German aviation began massive air strikes on the tank corps and these activities reached their peak on July 16. *Luftwaffe* aircraft flying in groups of fifteen to twenty and sometimes forty aircraft bombed the Soviet columns from the morning until the late evening, while the intervals between attacking aircraft sections was now a mere thirty minutes.

As a result of twelve air strikes on July 16, the 1st Tank Corps lost seven T-34, seven T-70, 17 BA-64, 49 armoured cars, two armoured personnel carriers, nine motorcycles and one radio set, while the anti-aircraft artillery regiment, attached to the corps, had only four cannon remaining. The 5th Tank Corps also suffered heavy damages, and all its radio sets were put out of order. Soviet fighter cover was 'passive' to say the least and the tank crews saw only one fighter, an La-5, which made an emergency landing! When analysing the activities of the enemy's aviation, the headquarters of the 1st Air Army noted: 'Where our ground troops were having a success, or in locations where our motorized units were moving to the theatre of operations, the enemy immediately threw in large numbers of bombers. In July operations, the Ju 87 dive bombers were active in large quantities, and were the real threat to our troops'.

During 17–18 July, the German attack and anti-tank units made low-level strikes on the motorised columns of the 1st Tank Corps. Hs 129's firing their anti-tank 30m cannon hit an average of eight to ten tanks per day and the 89th Tank Brigade suffered the most from these strikes – with only nine tanks left serviceable by July 20. German *General* H. Plocher noted these events: "The units of the 1st German Air Division, supported by fighters, dive bombers and anti-tank aviation, which were relocated to the Orel area

from the positions of the 8th Air Corps in the Southern sector of the Kursk area, attacked the Russian forces with bombs and with the fire of their small-calibre cannon. Their efforts were concentrated against a large tank formation, which had moved out of the forest to open territory and tried to cross the Bryank-Orel railway line in the vicinity of Khotinet. This railway was the major route for supporting the ground troops defending Orel. There were no German reserves in this area which could repel the attack, but the Luftwaffe units forced the Russian tanks to stop.

The German command used all available units of anti-tank and ground attack aviation for delivering air strikes against enemy troops, and especially the tanks, flying from early morning until late in the evening. Hundreds of tanks were destroyed by air attacks. When the Russians intended to continue their spurt to Khotinets under the cover of the night, the Germans managed to relocate the division of anti-aircraft artillery from Karachaevo to this area. During two days the Luftwaffe units, without support of ground troops, managed to keep control over the Bryank-Orel railway line and destroyed most of the Russian tanks which broke through. *Generaloberst* W. Model noted in a telegram: "For the first time in the history of the war, the Luftwaffe, without the support of ground troops, deprived the fighting ability of a Russian tank brigade."

Since the early days of the Soviet counter-offensive, German reconnaissance aircraft closely monitored the movements of large formations of tanks. This was not always easy as the tank corps and armies were covered by anti-aircraft artillery regiments, and quite often supported by patrolling fighters. On July 16, a Ju 88D of 4(F)./121 piloted by the unit commander *Hauptmann* E. von der Ropp was shot down over the 10th Tank Corps and the next day, another aircraft of the same unit, piloted by Leutnant E. Keller, did not return to its base – being shot down near Efremov – the crew becoming POWs. The crew was interrogated and described the German practice of using different types of aircraft for reconnaissance, and in order to improve their tactical knowledge they received additional training about the structure of the Soviet tank forces, the main types of tanks and their weaknesses. In particular, this crew was monitoring the movements from Plavsk of the 3rd Guards Tank Army commanded by General P.S. Rybalko and this unit was actively bombed by the Germans on 20 July. With the same difficulties as the 3rd Guards Tank Army (initially fighting on the left flank of the Bryansk Front) the 4th Tank Army, headed by General V.M. Badanov, was advancing on the right flank. Under heavy fire from the Luftwaffe, the army literally 'gnawed' through the well organised German anti-tank defenses at Bolkhov, and after eighteen days had lost almost 84% of its T-34s and 46% of T-70s.

If the Soviet command had been able to detect the strong points of the enemy's defences and bypass them then the results of operation 'Kutuzov' might have been different. The greatest successes obtained by the *Luftwaffe* were when attacking the motorised units which had entered the breakthrough gap. In the report of July 26 to Stalin, Marshall for Artillery N.N. Voronov summarised the experience of the break-through of German defences at the Bryansk and Western Fronts. He paid attention to the activity of aviation, and actually acknowledged the serious threat to Soviet ground troops from the *Luftwaffe*. He also noted that although there was a three-fold numerical superiority it was insufficient for air dominance over the main battle areas: "In locations where it is expected to achieve a break-through and reach considerable operational success, it is necessary to enter, sooner or later, into large-scale air engagement. The issue of paramount importance is the quantity of our fighter aviation. We need fighters for reliable air cover for the advancing troops, motorised units, for covering day bomber strikes, attack aircraft and artillery spotting aviation. The experience of battles at the Orel sector shows that the enemy to a large extent hindered the

⌖ Soviet officers observe the Junkers of StG2 shot down near Orel.

⌖ A Ju 88 of 6./KG51 in flight. Note the MG-FF machine gun, installed in the belly canoe.

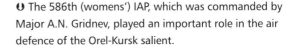

⌖ The 586th (womens') IAP, which was commanded by Major A.N. Gridnev, played an important role in the air defence of the Orel-Kursk salient.

⌖ A new Hs 129 ground attack aircraft is being prepared for the battle near Kursk.

⋂ Soviet and French pilots of the 303rd IAD discuss the results of combat sorties.

⋂ Lieutenant J. Leon from the 'Normandie' squadron takes off in his Yak-1 from an airfield in the vicinity of Orel. End of July 1943.

⋂ Crew of M. Albert (later on HSU). Left to right: technician A. Averyanov, French pilot, armourer M. Mamaev.

⋂ An American M3 medium tank, supplied to the USSR under the Lend-Lease agreement, destroyed by artillery fire and air strikes.

activity of our troops by using its air force. The Germans gathered their main aviation forces in this area, so it was the place for us to give a general air battle to the enemy. In my opinion, we should have had up to 1,000 fighter planes for three fronts. The experience of battles shows that Tigers and Ferdinands do not scare our ground troops, but the enemy's aviation has a strong morale-sapping effect. Very often it slows down the pace of our advance. We should pay more attention to the anti-aircraft artillery and fighter cover than we have done before...".

For delivering air strikes on the Soviet ground troops, the Germans widely used not only dive bombers and attack aircraft, but heavy bombers as well. According to the opinion of the *Luftwaffe* command, such activity assisted in the successful retreat of the ground troops to the West, but resulted in unjustified losses of aircraft and well trained crews of the 6th Air Fleet. For example, II./KG53, which arrived from Germany on July 15, had forty-five

He 111s on strength and the same number of combat-ready crews. However by July 31, only thirty-seven bombers (twenty-five combat ready) remained.

The Germans withdraw to the Hagen line

From July 22 the commanders at the Central Front made several attempts to expand the offensive in the north. At that time the main strikes moved from the right to the left flank, which was strengthened then by the 2nd Tank Army by the end of July. Some success in the early stage of the operation can be inferred from Stalin's interference in the situation and the transfer of the 3rd Guards Tank Army to the command of General K.K. Rokossovsky. In the last few days of July the weather was poor and the Headquarters of Commander in Chief ordered the transfer of part of the aviation forces (the 2nd IAK, 11th Mixed Air Corps [SAK], and 224th ShAD) plus ground troops from the Western Front to the Bryansk Front. General V.D. Sokolovsky received instructions to start preparations for the

'Smolensk' offensive operation as his troops were no longer participating in the counter-offensive near Kursk. The task of finally destroying the enemy group was now to be completed by the Central and Bryansk Fronts, together with the 16th and 15th Air Armies with support of some units from Long-Range Aviation.

In the early morning of August 1, the reconnaissance aircraft of both air armies spotted the retreat of German truck columns and tanks from Orel to Bryansk. They noted some 500–1,000 trucks and cars, which were moving in a continuous column with German fighters on hand. The Commander of the Red Army Air Force, Marshal A.A. Novikov personally ordered commanders of the 15th and 16th Air Armies to carry out day and night air strikes across this withdrawal, so Soviet attack aircraft, in groups of four to six Il-2s, bombed and fired on troops and vehicles from low level. On August 1, one eight-aircraft formation of Pe-2 bombers destroyed fifteen trucks, a fact later confirmed by aerial reconnaissance. The roads were now littered with burning cars, trucks and armoured vehicles, with the German command making every effort to blunt the attack of the Red Army and to pull their troops back to the Hagen line. As noted in German reports, units of the 1st Air Division, whilst providing air cover for retreating forces, carried out 3,241 sorties on 1–2 August, entering into dozens of dogfights. According to their data, about 150 Soviet tanks were destroyed in these air raids, allowing the Germans to save the 7th, 258th and 31st Rifle Divisions from complete destruction.

In fact, the 9th Tank Corps of the 2nd Tank Army indeed suffered heavy losses and the Deputy Commander of the Corps, General-Mayor Bakharov, was wounded, while the brigade commanders Colonels Boyarinov and Galushko were badly shaken. On August 2 alone, about 840 enemy aircraft attacked, destroying twenty-three T-34 and sixteen T-70 tanks with seventy troops and sixty-five wounded. Along with the German aircraft, the units were mistakenly bombed by Soviet aviation (there were no communication between the 9th Tank Corps and 16th Air Army), and that worsened the situation even further! On the previous day, the 16th Air Army attacked the German troops which were withdrawing from the Orel bridgehead, stopping any formation on the west bank of the Kroma. In one of the bomb strikes to the south-west of Orel the commander of the 46th Tank Corps, General H. von Zorn, was fatally wounded, and on the same day fighters of the 15th Air Army were very close to eliminating *Generalfeldmarschall* H. von Kluege when his Fieseler Storch was attacked by Soviet fighters to the south-east of Karachev, and made a forced landing. Although injured, Kluege continued to command the troops and under his orders the Germans withdrew from Orel on August 5. When retreating, they blew up all the roads across Oka River, as well as many military and civil facilities in the city.

The average daily losses of the 6th SAK in the beginning of August were about three to five aircraft, however, on the morning of August 5, the aces of IV./JG51, headed by *Oberleutnant* H.G. von Fassong, intercepted a group of Bostons and shot down eight of their number plus one fighter in 15 minutes of air

☾ The famous German pilot Hans-Ulrich Rudel shows how to attack Soviet tanks. In the course of the defence battles near Orel he carried out his 1,200th sortie.

☝ A German armourer loads the ammunition for an MK 103 cannon. In the course of the battle these cannon were successfully used on Hs 129 attack aircraft.

combat. Also in the first part of August Soviet fighter regiments which had participated in the battles on the Central Front began to wear victory markings, and much success was achieved by the pilots of the 67th GvIAP pf the 1st GvIAD. During almost all of July, this regiment equipped with Airacobras was in the reserves of the Commander of the 16th Air Army. When the air battle intensified, the unit was brought into combat and scored fifty-two victories from the 1–4 August.

One of the unquestionable successes was shooting down the Commander of I./JG54, *Major* G. Homuth, in an air battle on August 3. German dive bombers also suffered considerable losses. On August 4 the pilots of the 157th IAP, led by Commander Mayor V.F. Volkov, bravely attacked a large group of Ju 87s and in the course of the battle between twelve Yak-7Bs and fifty Junkers right over the bridge across Kroma river, the Soviet pilots claimed twelve victories. They also reported that most of the dive bombers released their loads before reaching the target. Among the highest scorers of the 6th IAK was the Squadron Commander of the 347th IAP Senior Lieutenant L.K. Ryzhy, who shot down five and damaged two aircraft during two

days of battles. Elements of his success were attributed to his coolness and the 37mm cannon of his Yak-9T, which he named a 'Howitzer'. According to German records, the StG1 alone lost about twenty Ju 87s from 2 to 4 August and despite massive strikes by the *Luftwaffe*, by the end of August 4 the Soviet troops had reached the banks of Kroma River and crossed it in several places. When spotting the Russian tanks on the northern bank of the river the German command again brought into action its attack aviation; on the morning of August 5 the 6th Guards Tank Corps of the 3rd Tank Army was attacked by formations of up to forty aircraft. The 106th Tank Brigade lost four tanks in this air strike and the tank crews retreated to the southern bank of the river.

Against the triumphant liberation of Orel on August 5 by the troops of the Bryansk Front, the situation in the area, under the responsibility of General K.K. Rokossovsky, was far from bright and losses were high. In his order issued on the following day Rokossovsky wrote: 'The 3rd Guards Tank Army and the 2nd Tank Army, despite the favorable situation and contrary to my orders, did not fulfill the given tasks and dawdled at the same place for three days. This was the result of the fact

U Armament technicians load up an Il-2 attack aircraft.

O A technician repairs the M-11 engine of a U-2 light bomber.

⋂ Senior Lieutenant S.K. Kalinichenko was one of the highest scoring pilots of the 519th IAP, and all 283rd IAD. He did not return from a combat sortie on 30 August 1943, and was posthumously awarded with the star of HSU.

⋂ The trucks of a German column on fire after an attack by Soviet aviation.

that the commanders of tank units experience uncertainty, cannot force their subordinates to fulfill the tasks and poorly control the units during combat'. On August 9, after fierce battles, the 2nd Tank Army was withdrawn to the rear, and was followed by the 3rd Guards Tank Army by the end of the following day. This army during several days of the battle lost around 100 tanks, and by August 11 the 7th Guards Tank Corps had only four T-34s and seven T-70s in serviceable condition. Soviet losses in the air, however, had decreased considerably, but on 7 August the Commander of the 63rd GvIAP Lieutenant Colonel N.P. Ivanov was killed in the air battle (he was posthumously awarded with the Star of Hero of Soviet Union).

The Soviet units were also considerably weakened by the inflicted losses and this resulted in slowing the pace of following the retreating enemy. However, some of the Soviet aviation units were still able to carry out successful combat as, for example, on August 12 the 3rd ShAK was mounting strikes on the German troops defending Karachev, and undertook 114 sorties in spite of the heavy anti-aircraft fire and the activity of German fighters. Thanks to the thorough preparations for each flight, the allocation of a unit for suppressing the Flak positions and reliable air cover by fighters, the

losses were kept to a minimum. On the same day the Soviet ground troops liberated Dmitrievsk-Orlovsky and moved 12km in the direction of Karachev. Karachev was an important strong point and was abandoned on August 15, while on the next day the Red Army entered Zhizdra. However, the Soviet forces could not break through the Hagen positions straight away, and on August 18 the Central and Bryansk Fronts turned to defence.

The strain of air combat went down noticeably and as well as the successes a lot of shortcomings during operation 'Kutuzov' had been noted. Aviation support in the breakthrough areas of large tank formations was not always well prepared, nor air strikes on the enemy's reserves efficient, and coordination between the aviation elements and the ground troops suffered from significant flaws. Due to the latter reason, unexpectedly heavy losses during the final stage of the operation were experienced by Il-4 bombers of the 113th BAD which lost thirty-seven aircraft in August. Among the crews lost were the Commander of the 836th BAP Lieutenant Colonel Pobogin and Squadron Commander of the 815th BAP Major Lyakh.

Chapter 6
War in the night sky

In course of the battles in the Kursk area, intensive air combat took place not only in the day, but at night as well. From the first day of the battle night raids were carried out by units of the 208th Night Bomber Air Division (NBAD) of the 2nd Air Army and the 271st NBAD of the 16th Air Army, which were equipped with U-2 and R-5 aircraft. By that time, the German command had already established opponents for the Soviet night bombers – in the shape of four or five *Störkampfstaffel* night light-attack aircraft units. These units were equipped with trainers or with outdated types such as the He 46, Ar 66, Go 145, Hs 126 and others. The main task for the night bomber units was to exhaust the enemy's troops, and to them keep awake by constant harassment. Also the Long Range Aviation (ADD) elements took an active part in the night battles.

By the beginning of July 1943 the ADD had 740 (523 serviceable) bombers and 697 crews, with 628 of them trained for operations at night. The most numerous aircraft type in service was the Il-4 (DB-3f) with a total of 397 bombers in the 1st, 2nd and 3rd Guards Air Corps, 50th Air Division of the 6th Air Corps, and 36th Air Division. The Li-2 was also in service with four air division: the 1st, 12th, 53rd, 62nd, with other aircraft from the 54th Air Division (in total 199 aircraft). The latter unit also had on its strength thirty-two outdated TB-3 bombers, many of which

were built early in the 1930s. The 4th Guards Air Corps was equipped with eighty-eight American B-25 Mitchell bombers and six Er-2 aircraft. Finally, the 45th Air Division had eighteen (eleven serviceable) four-engined Pe-8 bombers.

The ADD units applied most of their efforts to supporting troops in the Kursk area, as well as continuing to make air strikes on the ports at the Black Sea, which were occupied by Germans. In the first half of July about 350–400 aircraft were in combat every night, and bombed concentrations of German troops and equipment. The ADD losses for this period were fifteen aircraft but in the face of German anti-aircraft fire this increased considerably. It turned out that the Germans especially strengthened the areas around Orel, Bryansk, and Belgorod with anti-aircraft units, especially around the main railway junctions, and moved in additional 88mm Flak cannon and searchlights. According to Soviet intelligence data, before the Kursk battle units of the 12th and 18th anti-aircraft divisions, which covered the areas of Orel and Bryansk, had been strengthened and in addition to the known Würzburg and Freya radars, the Germans began to utilise Wassermann radar, used for controlling anti-aircraft fire.

A specific feature of the anti-aircraft defence at the Eastern Front was the installation of radar equipment onto railway flatcars, which provided a highly mobile

◖ Il-4 long-range night bombers line up for take-off. In some phases of the Kursk battle these planes were also used for day missions.

◖ U-2 night light bombers on their way to the target.

↻ Mitchells of the 4th GvBAK in combat. In the beginning of August 1943 this unit bombed the railway stations of Bryansk, Karachev, Merefa, Poltava and Krasnograd.

system. It was also known that several night fighters of the IV./NJG5 were equipped with Lichtenstein radars. On the eve of the counteroffensive at the Bryansk Front, almost all units of the ADD (except for the 6th Air Corps) were bombing the resistance points in this area. After taking off at sunset, 360 aircraft made a raid on German strong points to the west of Novosil, while 189 aircraft bombed the second line of defence, along with artillery positions and enemy reserves to the south-west of Kozelsk. Because of fierce fighting on the ground, the front line was clearly visible from the air, so the crews found their targets precisely. When it became clear that the Soviet counter-attack in the vicinity of Prokhorovka had not brought the desired result and the situation at the southern end of the Kursk area became critical, most of the heavy bombers started to attack on the Voronezh Front. The targets here were primarily the tank units of *Generalfeldmarschall* Erich von Manstein. Marshall Vasilevskiy thus ordered the units to use high-calibre bombs, not only to eliminate troops and equipment, but also to subdue morale.

On the night of July 13 long-range aviation made only a limited number of sorties due to bad weather conditions, but on the next night it made up some leeway – as out of an available 116 Il-4, Li-2, and TB-3

aircraft, 108 aircraft bombed a concentration of troops, the headquarters, and the communication centres of the 4th German Panzer Army and other units. According to the opinion of the ADD command, the precise bombing of the targets was achieved thanks to the accurate illumination by 'pathfinders' of the 2nd Air Corps including pilots V.V. Sapozhnikov, V.M. Bezbokov, and S.S. Apukhtin (all of them being ex-pilots of the Civil Air Fleet). Then, for several of the following days the main efforts were directed to Orel, and in addition to the main railway junction the aircraft bombed Mokhovaya railway station, a concentration of troops in Bolkhov, and enemy columns on the roads from Orel to the north and west. "The anti-aircraft defence of Orel put our pilots on edge" recalled A.M. Krsnukhin. "Many of us had been familiar with it earlier, but at this time it was more intense, with up to twenty searchlights lighting the sky, and anti-aircraft artillery with middle and large calibre weapons fiercely firing at our aircraft".

On the night of July 18 almost all ADD units were attacking the transportation system, railway junctions, stations and large roads. More than 700 aircraft were in the air, and about half of them were working on the South-Western Front. For the first time all the units from long-range aviation were brought into action and

His comrades congratulate Captain A.A. Alekhnovich of the 6th GvBAP (1st GgBAK) with the completion of his 200th combat sortie.

Bombs are being prepared for lifting under a Pe-8 of the 45th Air Division. During the whole war this aircraft type was the most powerful and heaviest series production bomber in Soviet service.

Long-range Ilyushin bombers in a combat sortie.

the German command was forced to manoeuvre its reserves. The primary transportation routes for the Germans remained the railway lines, so the this became the primary task for the 1st Guards, 5th and 7th Air Corps, 36th and 45th Air Divisions of the ADD (in total about 300 bombers). According to the reports of the Soviet aviators, considerable damage was inflicted on the railway stations at Navlya, Karachaev and Orel and the 6th Air Fleet managed to put up fourteen night fighters which shot down seven Soviet bombers, according to German records. Also that night A.I. Kalentyev of the 7th Guards Air Regiment of the 53rd Air Division was doing his eighty-seventh combat sortie flying a TB-3 when he failed to spot the approach of an enemy fighter – and the German pilot managed to set fire to the heavy bomber, which fell down to the north of Karachev station, but thankfully all crew members safely bailed out.

The crew of another TB-3 piloted by V.M. Bezbokov spotted the parachutes and landed in the nearest corn field and rescued the crew of the shot-down TB-3. The crew members of a second shot-down TB-3 flown by V.K. Pirushevtsev of the 325th TBAP of the same division were not so lucky – only two air gunners managed to escape from the falling bomber. According to German sources, before dawn the fighters of IV./NJG5 made seventeen sorties and scored twelve victories, with seven of them allocated *Hauptmann* H. zu Sain Wittgenstein. In his 'free hunting' nocturnal raids he used two Ju 88C-6s – one aircraft was a standard series production aircraft equipped with radar, while the second had the underfuselage container removed and the wing leading edge polished, so its maximum speed was increased by 40 km/h.

Pe-8 in the gunsight

In the late evening of July 14, and not far from Orel, a Pe-8 bomber commanded by the Seniour Lieutenant N.I. Sushin was set on fire and crashed to the ground, while on the night of July 21 three other Pe-8 bombers (serial numbers 42049, 42058, and 42109) did not return to their base. These were flown by very experienced pilots – Major A. Vikhorev of the 890th Air Regiment, Major V.V. Ponomarenko and Captain Ugryumov (both of the 746th Air Regiment). It was later revealed they had been attacked by German 'hunters' to the north-east of Orel. Such heavy losses had not been experienced before and were never repeated. Out of thirty-four crew members seventeen managed to cross the front line and return in a small groups or one by one. Among the MIA was the 'pathfinder' Lieutenant Colonel A.M. Lebedev – one of the most experienced navigators of Long-Range Aviation, who carried out 180 combat sorties, including two missions over Berlin.

Usually, successful attacks by German fighters were the ones which were unexpected by Pe-8 crews. One such example was a mission commanded by Major A. Vikharev. Vikharev, in spite of being caught in four-five German searchlights and heavy Flak, was able to carry out his bombing run from 5,750m, and then put the aircraft into a sharp slide at high speed, and managed to fly out of the searchlight. In about a minute the crew heard heavy pounding on the right wing, which became immediately on fire. The commander ordered the crew to bail out as he was sure that the aircraft had been hit by anti-aircraft fire. However, a splinter of a 20mm cannon round, which a surgeon removed from the leg of wounded navigator Alekseev, evidenced that it was a German fighter that had scored the victory. Another aircraft, commanded by M.M. Ugryumov, was shot down in the same circumstances, as when returning to base the cabins of the flight technician and radio operators were set on fire, a blaze which quickly spread throughout the aircraft.

An unseen night fighter had made an attack from the front hemisphere slightly lower than the bomber, which had limited visibility and was poorly defended in this area. These meant that the German pilots knew its weak points and had capitalised on this with deadly effect. According to German records, these Pe-8s were shot down by *Hauptmann* H. zu Sain Wittgenstein, and on the evening of July 22 he also set fire to an aircraft flown by P.I Nemkov, killing all the crew. Later on it became clear that the German command had obtained information from captured Soviet crews about the Pe-8, its combat formations and methods of bombing, which had not changed for several months. The shorter July nights did not allow the Soviet command to change the times of an air strike, and they continued to deliver them about an hour before midnight, always from a north-easterly direction, thus making it easy for the Germans to anticipate a raid. Also the shot-down Pe-8s were powered by new M-82 engines, which had no exhaust flame dumpers, so were relatively easy to spot at night. The crews were recommended to increase the bombing altitude and to 'compact' flight formations as much as possible. The commander of the 45th Air Division Colonel V. Lebedev also noted that all three Pe-8s shot down had approached the target area with a considerable separation from other aircraft in the formation, which probably simplified the enemy's ability to direct its fighters.

Successes and losses

Such a heavy losses started to worry the Soviet command and new tactics and countermeasures were prepared. It was noted that the German fighters usually patrolled the area in pairs at high altitude, outside the area of fire of anti-aircraft artillery, and periodically sent light signals to each other. In some cases one of the German fighters switched on its navigation and landing lights, intentionally attracting attention of the bomber crews, while the other fighter, unseen, approached the bomber and dispatched it. When the Flak crews suddenly ceased fire and changed direction, this was a signal to the bomber crews that it was a time to increase vigilance and await an attack any minute. Initially the German night fighters also preferred to attack bombers from the rear hemisphere, but now the favorite direction was from below as such engagements revealed the poor survivability of many Soviet aircraft types, including Pe-8, and poor quality self-sealing fuel tanks. On July 20 the Soviet command expanded its area of active combat, and forced the Germans to relocate their

⋒ The famous night fighter pilot *Hauptmann* H. zu Sain Wittgenstein at the Eastern front. During the Kursk battle he commanded IV./NJG5, which in the beginning of August 1943 was renamed as the new NJG100.

reserves from one region of battle to another. After the offensive on the Southern and South-Western Fronts on July 22 the troops in the Leningrad and Volhkov Fronts increased their activities. The ADD units participated in the operations in all locations, from the Far North to the Black Sea. High hopes were placed on them by the Commander-in-Chief Headquarters in the operation near Leningrad, where the Germans had created powerful defences.

On the night of August 6 the 4th Guards Air Corps made ninety-eight sorties attacking the railway lines in the Bryansk area. The mission control officer, Major V.A. Gordilovsky, noted some 126 hits, and about an hour before midnight heavy fighting took place between B-25 bombers and Ju 88C night fighters. Three Soviet aircraft and one German fighter were shot down, and six Soviet crew members and three German aviators perished. The Germans had by that time also reorganised their night fighter aviation on the Eastern Front. From August 1 IV./NJG5 was renamed as I./NJG100, while the 10th, 11th, and 12th *Staffeln* became the 1st, 2nd, and 3rd *Staffeln* and it was planned to establish a full scale *Geschwader*, NJG100, from the crews operating with radar direction support. In the second half of the month, NJG200 was formed from the night fighter flights of different Air Fleets, and it was expected that the pilots from this unit would be carrying out 'free hunting' night combat and be flown by aircraft equipped with FuG212 Lichtenstein radars.

German night fighter pilots reported about ninety Soviet aircraft shot down July–August with the highest scoring pilots of IV./NJG5 being *Hauptmanns* A. Lechner, A. Fenske and *Oberleutnant's* H. Gref and R. Landau. It should be noted that Soviet reports in summer 1943 mention the Bf 110 as the main type of German night fighter and in fact, this type was on the strength of 11./NJG5, which was operating from the airfields of Poltava and Stalino. Night bombers flying over Orel, Bryansk, Seshcha and other towns in the northern sector of the Kursk area were intercepted

mostly by Ju 88Cs, which were in service with the 10th and 12th units of the same NJG5. Along with the Junkers, Do 217J and N versions were used, which were not popular with crews. New group commander, *Hauptmann* R. Schoenert, as well as *Oberleutnant* R. Rathke were among the few pilots who mastered this type and successfully used its powerful armament. However, most of the pilots were sceptical of the Dornier's capabilities in the night fighter role, naming it the 'slow crow' due to its insufficient airspeed and poor manoeuvrability. However, the impression that the German side was only defending in the night air battle is not correct. During the 'Zitadelle' offensive the most frequent bombing attacks were carried out by German aircraft hitting railway stations at Kursk-Stariy Oskol, as well as Valuyki stations. These air raids were mainly carried out by Ju 88A and C versions of II./KG3.

When the group was relocated from Poltava to Bryansk they continued to carry out night missions on the railways. Thus, on the night of July 17 the units of the 6th Air Fleet made 289 combat sorties, with 206 of them bombing, and the crews of III./KG1, II./KG3, II./KG51, and III./KG4, trained for night raids, bombed near Ulyanovo and Krapivino and suppressed anti-aircraft artillery positions, and flew 'free hunting' missions against the trains on the Mtsensk-Tula-Sukhinichi-Gorbachevo lines. According to the debriefing interviews of *Luftwaffe* pilots, at least five trains were derailed. Some of the German attacks were recorded in Soviet documents. For example, on the morning of July 31, while bombing Volosta station (25 km to the south of Vyazma) thirty-three Ju 88s and eleven He 111s dropped around 300 HE bombs, including twenty-five 1,000 kg bombs, and as a result thirty men were killed and fifty wounded, 1,000m of track was destroyed as was one steam engine, and a truck with ammunition exploded. The documents also mention the German attempts to block the airfields used by the Long-Range Aviation aircraft, when separate Heinkels of 14./KG27 patrolled for quite a long

↻ A U-2 biplane is being prepared for a night sortie.

↻ A Tiger tank crew observe Soviet night planes appearing in the false dawn.

♩ Commander of the 19th GvIAP HSU Colonel V.G. Tikhonov sets the task for the combat mission. Left to right: Captain V.V. Reshetnikov, Captain P.P. Khrustalev, Lieutenant Colonel P.P. Radchuk, Senior Lieutenant V.F. Roshchenko.

time near Morozovsk, dropping one or two bombs at a time in order to impede take-off and landing of the aircraft of the 62nd Air Division.

However, the ADD units were keeping up their high intensity operations, and improved their tactics. In August 1943 the strikes on the targets were arranged in such a way that routes, altitudes and target approaches were changed, thus avoiding the templates. When carrying out bomb strikes on important objects with the forces of a single, or several corps, so-called 'star-raids' were utilised – approaches now primarily being made from the direction of the German rear. Also each regiment received its own bomb dropping altitudes, and locations of crossing the front-line were selected where the probability of meeting the German night fighters was minimal. Flight Technician N.M. Gornostaev from the 102nd Air Regiment of the 7th Air Corps recalled his bombing mission on Unecha station, while flying in the crew of Captain V.A. Tishko in an Li-2 bomber: "When the pilot dropped the HE bombs from the underwing bomb racks, I took my turn. I ran to the cargo cabin, opened the door, and dragged the boxes with the small bombs closer to the opening. I was dropping the bombs, and the aircraft was tossing around because of the heavy explosions on the ground.

Then, firmly fixing myself against the fuselage side, tightening my safety strap I looked at the results of our work though the open door – the bombs burst like strange flowers right in the middle of the trains parked at the station. Suddenly a deadly white light of the searchlight blinded me. 'They caught us – bastards' – I thought and shut the door. At this moment I heard the voice of our gunner Pavel Radchenko in the intercom – 'I see a fighter, commander'. A line of tracer rounds crossed the window as our machine-guns returned the fire, I heard the sound of the falling cartridges, the cabin became full of powder smoke. The plane was turning sharply to the right and descending – I thought we were shot down, but our Li-2 pulled out of its dive near the ground and the searchlight lost us". After landing it turned out that a shell of the German fighter had damaged the outer wing panel, but this was repaired the next day. Two other aircraft were damaged that night, and the Li-2 of Lieutenant V.A. Kazyonov was shot down by Flak. The German command tried to intensify their night operations but their fighters could not paralyze the operations of the Red Army aviation and ADD.

Chapter 7
The Red Army advances to Kharkov

Being unable to break through the Soviet defensive positions at the Southern edge of the Kursk area, on 17–18 July the German command turned to defence. They tried to hold the Belgorod-Kharkov bulge, which was considered 'the bastion, closing the way for the Russian armies in their advance to the Ukraine'. The commander of Army Group 'South' *Generalfeldmarschall* Erich von Manstein decided to retreat his troops to the positions from where the Germans had began the 'Zitadelle' offensive on July 5.

The Germans turn to defence

The most powerful centres of German resistance were now at Belgorod, Kharkov, Tomarovka, Akhtyrka and Bogodukhov. Kharkov's defence was strengthened especially well – a powerful circle – which included heavy anti-tank and anti-aircraft armour well organised around the city. The most serious obstacle for the Soviet armies was Severskiy Donets River, but the extensive anti-aircraft artillery of the 10th, 15th, and 17th anti-aircraft defence divisions were ready not only to repel the attacks of Soviet aircraft, but also to participate in the ground battles. The Germans replenished their troops with personnel and materiel, using Ju 52 transports of I./TG3, II./TG3 and II./TG4 concentrated at Zhitomir airfield, and the airfields of Zaporozhye and Dnepropetrovsk noted the appearance of cargo gliders and many liaison and courier planes. In the second half of July, the German command relocated to the Orel bridgehead and Mius River six units including *Panzergrenadier Division Grossdeutchland, SS Panzergrenadier Division Leibstandarte Adolf Hitler, SS Panzergrenadier Division Das Reich* and the *SS Panzergrenadier Division Totenkop* which played a key role in attacking Kursk from south. In opposition, the Soviet troops were notably strengthened when the forces

↻↺ One of the airfields after withdrawal of German forces. In the foreground – an He 111 destroyed during an air raid by Soviet attack aircraft (below and opposite top and bottom).

of the Stepnoy Front entered the main battle area.

At the end of July – beginning of August, certain events took place which should be mentioned. The German command managed to temporarily stabilise the front at Mius River after repositioning ground troops and strengthening the 4th Air Corps with units of the 8th Air Corps. The Germans at first stopped the Soviet offensive, and then a powerful counter-strike eliminated the bridgehead on the western bank of the Mius River. Summarising the results of the battle the High Command noted the important role played by the Luftwaffe in supporting the ground troops. At the same time, the situation the air battles in the West was not so favourable for the Germans. Powerful strikes by British and American bombers on the industrial centres

⋂ Soviet troops in attack.

in Germany resulted in massive destruction and heavy losses of the civilian population.

On the night of July 25 a massive air attack was carried out on Hamburg and around 1,500 people died and most of the city was destroyed. The raid was repeated on July 28 and created an inferno in which about 50,000 people perished. The 8th US Air Force bombed Kiel, Hannover, Warnemünde, Kassel, and Hamburg as well. The air battles over Sardinia, Sicily and South Italy were lost by the Germans, and the combat losses in the Mediterranean in July 1943 exceeded the number of *Luftwaffe* losses at the Eastern front. All these factors forced the German Headquarters to rethink the positioning of its air units, and to strengthen the aviation forces in the west at the cost of weakening the Eastern Front. Thus at the end of July heavy fighter group I./ZG1 returned from Orel to Germany, to be followed by II./JG3 and III./JG3, relocated from the Donbass area to Holland. Thus, The Eastern Front lost more than 100 fighters and many experienced pilots.

The plan of the Soviet Command

Undoubtedly, the air combat situation in Belgorod-Kharkov area on the eve of the Soviet offensive favoured the Red Army Air Force. After the retreat of many German air units, which had been a part of the 8th Air Corps, to Donbass, air superiority was now in Soviet hands. At the beginning of August, the air corps, commanded by *General* H. Seidemann had only about 350 aircraft in service, including those from the 2nd Hungarian Air Brigade. Against them the Soviet command had the forces of the 2nd and 5th Air Armies, supported by the 17th Air Army and part of the ADD

forces. In total, these armies had 1,435 aircraft. The operational plan for the destruction of the Belgorod-Kharkov enemy group was given the name *Commander Rumyantsev*, and was being prepared by General Headquarters to be approved by the Commander-in-Chief Headquarters. The Soviet command wanted not only to cut the salient, but also to create the conditions for further liberation of the left-bank of the Ukraine and Donbass.

The following tasks were set for the aviation units:

A) To suppress and destroying the enemy's resistance points in the battlefield as well as at the concentration areas, to support the offensive of Soviet troops, and concentrate their main efforts in specific areas to breach the enemy's defence

B) To combat the activity of all types of aviation, to ensure the entrance of the tank units into the breakthrough areas and support their further advance

C) To maintain air superiority, and reliably cover the main groups on the fronts from the attention of enemy aviation, and to destroy the enemy's aircraft on the ground and in the air

D) By attacking railway lines and highways, to not allow the enemy's reserves to move to the battlefield

E) To carry out continuous air reconnaissance.

Based on the tasks set, the headquarters of the 2nd and 5th Air Armies planned aviation combat actions for the first day of the counter-offensive and according to these documents, the enemy's aircraft were to be destroyed in air combat only. In order to protect the troops from German aviation attacks, each air army

⋂ Commander of the 4th Air Fleet *General der Flieger* Otto Deßloch.

⋐ One of the young Soviet fighters in the cockpit of his Yak.

◑ La-5 fighter in flight. By the beginning of the battle at Orel-Kursk salient, the designers and production engineers managed to improve the performance of this aircraft type.

◑ A T-34 tank camouflaged in a haystack was almost impossible to spot from the air.

◑ Commander of the 2nd Air Army Lieutenant General S.A. Krasovsky.

was allocated one fighter air corps. Plans were also made to bomb the enemy's main lines in preparation for when the ground troops attacked. In order to support and cover the tanks during their breakthrough, the command of the 2nd and 5th Air Army was allocated forces from both fighter and attack aviation. In the course of the offensive, bombing aviation should carry out strikes on the nearest enemy reserves and restrict their advance to the battlefield. This task should have been performed mostly by the units of the 17th

Air Army and the ADD.

The headquarters of the 2nd Air Army, together with the headquarters of the general troops and tank armies, created a joint coded map, with which the pilots received their mission tasks. Another useful feature was the radio signal and communication chart, which was developed at the end of July for to connect the headquarters to ground troops and the command posts. Together with the artillerymen, the headquarters of the 2nd Air Army prepared a map of targets for the optimal

Lavochkin La-5FN 'White 04' serial number 39210104, 13th IAP, 201st IAD

Flown by Junior Lieutenant A.P. Druzhinin. The aircraft is painted in the colours standard for this fighter type in the first half of the war: AMT-4 green with AMT-6 black blotches on upper surfaces, and AMT-7 light blue on lower surfaces. Red stars have no trim.

Lavochkin La-5FN 'White 08', serial number 3921FN208, 92nd IAP, 279th IAD

Flown by Lieutenant Kononov. The aircraft is painted in the colours standard for this fighter type in the first half of the war: AMT-4 green with AMT-6 black blotches on upper surfaces, and AMT-7 light blue on lower surfaces. Red stars have no trim.

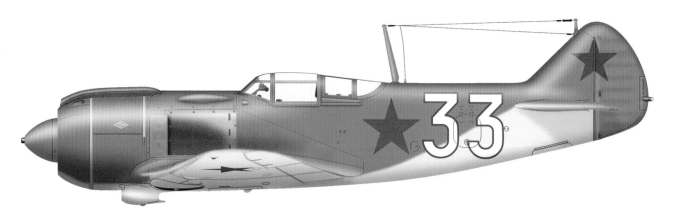

Lavochkin La-5FN 'White 33', Kursk, 1943

Flown by A.P. Maresyev. The aircraft is painted in non-standard camouflage for this period of the war: AMT-4 green upper surfaces and AMT-7 light blue lower surfaces. Large white tactical number, which was the characteristic feature of the La-5, has red trim. Red stars have no trim. Most likely, the aircraft underwent repairs, and the AMT-6 black paint was not available for restoring the blotches over the upper green.

Colour views by Andrey Yurgenson

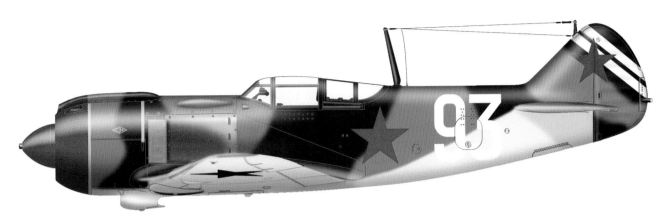

Lavochkin La-5FN 'White 93', 32nd GvIAP, 3rd GvIAD, 1st GvIAK, Kursk, summer 1943

Flown by Lieutenant V. Orekhov. The aircraft is painted in the colours standard for this fighter type in the first half of the war: AMT-4 green with AMT-6 black blotches on upper surfaces, and AMT-7 light blue on lower surfaces. Red stars have no trim. Note the red star victory marks painted under the canopy, red nose and two white bands on the rudder.

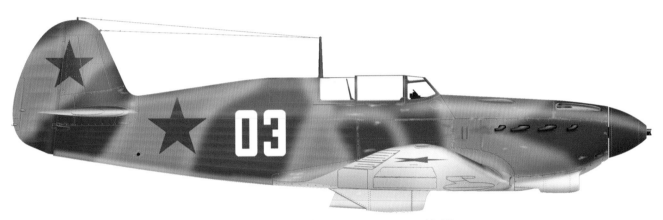

Yakolev Yak-7B 'White 03', 157th IAP, Kursk salient, summer 1943

Flown by the Squadron Commander Captain V.N. Zalevsky. The aircraft is painted in non-standard camouflage for this period of the war: the light brown bands are applied over the standard camouflage of AMT-4 green with AMT-6 black blotches on upper surfaces. The lower surfaces are painted in AMT-7 light blue. Red stars have no trim. Note the style of figure '3' which looks like the letter 'Э' of Russian alphabet, denoting the aircraft of the Sqn Cdr (Eskadrilya – Squadron – word starts with letter 'Э').

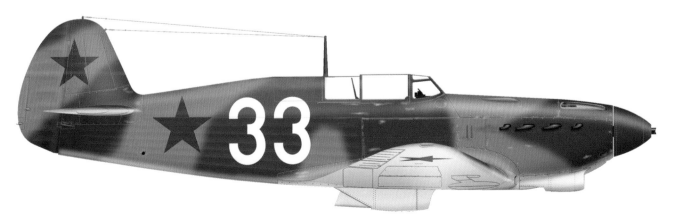

Yakolev Yak-7B 'White 33', 256th IAD, summer 1943

The aircraft is painted in the colours standard for this fighter type in the first half of the war: AMT-4 green with AMT-6 black blotches on upper surfaces, and AMT-7 light blue on lower surfaces. Red stars have no trim.

Colour views by Andrey Yurgenson

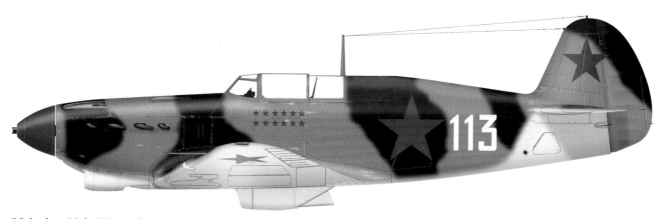

Yakolev Yak-7B 'White 113', summer 1943

The aircraft is painted in the colours standard for this fighter type in the first half of the war: AMT-4 green with AMT-6 black blotches on upper surfaces, and AMT-7 light blue on lower surfaces. Red stars have no trim. Note the red star victory marks painted under the canopy.

Yakolev Yak-7B 'White 26', 127th IAP, Kursk area, summer 1943

The aircraft is painted in the colours standard for this fighter type in the first half of the war: AMT-4 green with AMT-6 black blotches on upper surfaces, and AMT-7 light blue on lower surfaces. Red stars have no trim. Note the canopy having an improved field of view.

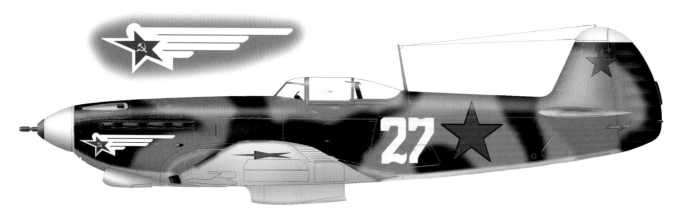

Yakolev Yak-9T 'White 27', 3rd Fighter Air Corps, Kursk area, summer 1943

The aircraft is painted in the colours standard for this fighter type in the first half of the war: AMT-4 green with AMT-6 black blotches on upper surfaces, and AMT-7 light blue on lower surfaces. Red stars have black trimming. Note white spinner with red tip.

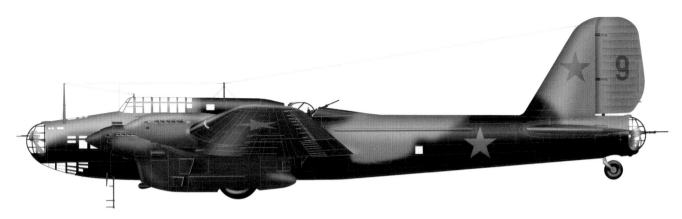

Petlyakov Pe-8 4AM-35 'Red 9', serial number 42028, summer 1943

746th Regiment of Long-Range Aviation. The aircraft is painted in the colours standard for this type in the first half of the war: AMT-4 green with AMT-6 black blotches on upper surfaces, and AMT-6 black on lower surfaces. Red stars have no trim.

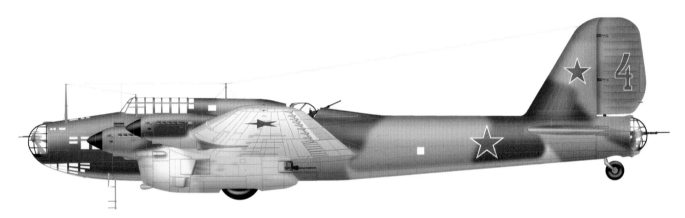

Petlyakov Pe-8 4AM-35 'Red 4', serial number 42082

746th Regiment of Long-Range Aviation. Three-tone camouflage of the upper surfaces is applied in accordance with the 'Camouflage Painting Scheme' of 1943, which includes green (AMT-4 or A-24m), light brown (AMT-1 or A-21m) and dark grey (AMT-12 or A-32m). The lower surfaces are painted in AMT-11 blue-grey. The stars and tactical number on the rudder have white trimming.

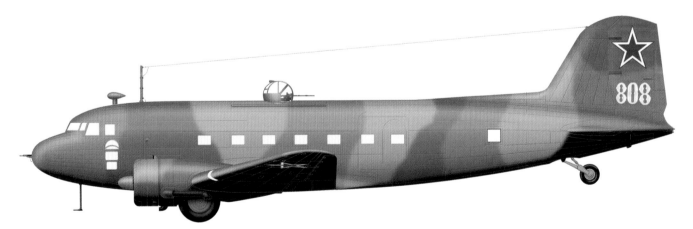

Li-2NB 'White 808', 62nd Division of Long-Range Aviation, 1943

Three-tone camouflage of the upper surfaces is applied in accordance with the 'Camouflage Painting Scheme' of 1943, which includes green (AMT-4 or A-24m), light brown (AMT-1 or A-21m) and dark grey (AMT-12 or A-32m). The lower surfaces are painted in AMT-6 black. Red stars have white/red trim.

Colour views by Andrey Yurgenson

Personal Li-2, 'White 9', of HSU V.M. Chistyakov, August 1943

The aircraft is painted in the colours standard for this type in the first half of the war: AMT-4 green with AMT-6 black blotches on upper surfaces, and AMT-7 light blue on lower surfaces. White inscription on the side reads *Ustyuzhanin* (citizen of Ustyug town).

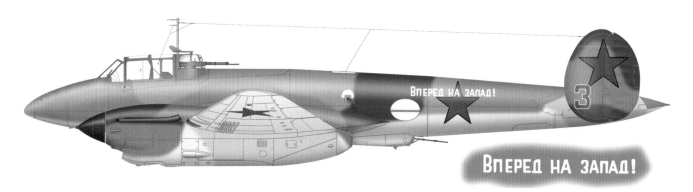

Pe-2 'Red 3', Kursk, summer 1943

Three-tone camouflage of the upper surfaces is applied in accordance with the 'Camouflage Painting Scheme' of 1943, which includes green (AMT-4 or A-24m), light brown (AMT-1 or A-21m) and dark grey (AMT-12 or A-32m). The lower surfaces are painted in AMT-11 blue-grey. The shape and size of black blotches differ from the standard variants 1 and 2, developed for Pe-2 bombers. The inscription on the fuselage reads 'Forward to the West!'

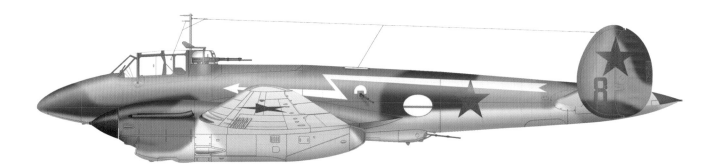

Petlyakov Pe-2 'Red 8', 511th RAR, 5th Air Army, Kursk, summer 1943

Three-tone camouflage of the upper surfaces is applied in accordance with the 'Camouflage Painting Scheme' of 1943, which includes green (AMT-4 or A-24m), light brown (AMT-1 or A-21m) and dark grey (AMT-12 or A-32m). The lower surfaces are painted in AMT-11 blue-grey. The shape and size of black blotches differ from the standard variants 1 and 2, developed for Pe-2 bombers. Note the white lightning bolt on the fuselage.

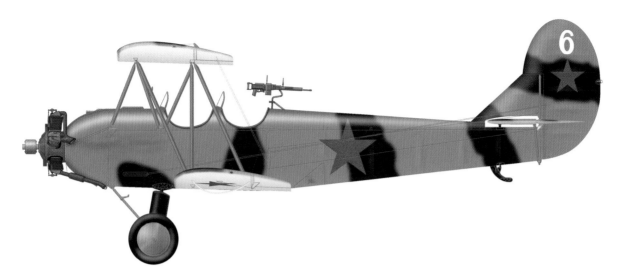

U-2VS 'White 6', 213th NBAD, summer 1943

The aircraft is painted in the colours standard for this type in the first half of the war: AMT-4 green with AMT-6 black blotches on upper surfaces, and AMT-7 light blue on lower surfaces.

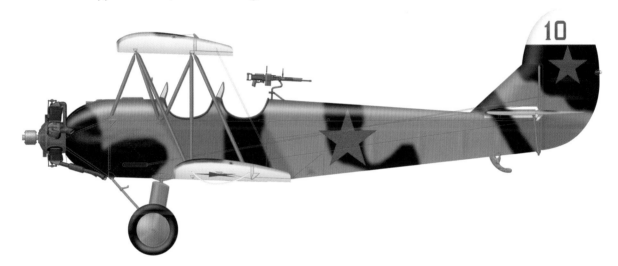

U-2VS 'White 10', 213th NBAD, summer 1943

The aircraft is painted in the colours standard for this type in the first half of the war: AMT-4 green with AMT-6 black blotches on upper surfaces, and AMT-7 light blue on lower surfaces. Note white rudder tip.

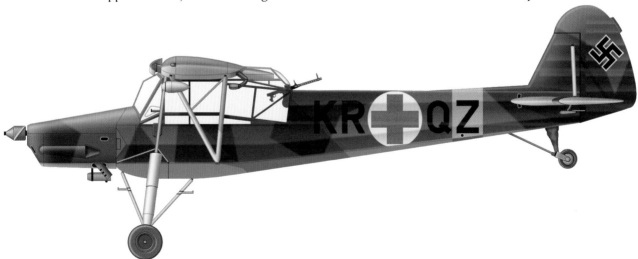

Fiesler Fi 156D, which belonged to the *Sanitäts-Bereitschaft Luftflotte* 6

The aircraft is camouflaged in a combination of RLM 70 (*Schwarzgrün*) and RLM 71 (*Dunkelgrün*) colours on upper surfaces. Lower surfaces are painted in RLM 65 (*Hellbrau* of 1941 standard).

Colour views by Andrey Yurgenson (U-2) and Mikhail Bykov (Fi 156)

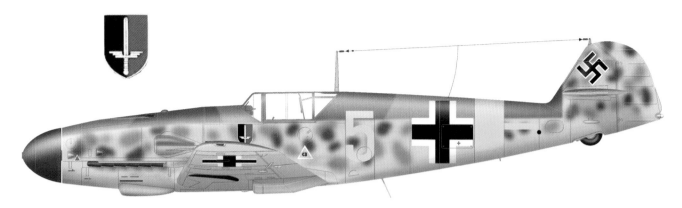

Messerschmitt Bf 109 'Yellow 5', II./JG52

Flown by *Staffelkapitän* Walter Krupinski. The fighter received standard factory camouflage of RLM 74 (*Dunkelgrau, grünlich*)/RLM 75 (*Mittelgrau*) on upper surfaces with blotches of RLM 70 (*Schwarzgrün*) and RLM 02 (RLM *Grau*). Lower surfaces are painted in RLM 76 (*Lichtblau*).

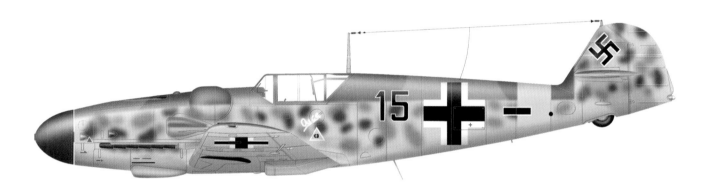

Messerschmitt Bf 109 'Black 15', II./JG52

The fighter received standard factory camouflage of RLM 74 (*Dunkelgrau, grünlich*)/RLM 75 (*Mittelgrau*) on upper surfaces with blotches of RLM 70 (*Schwarzgrün*) and RLM 02 (RLM *Grau*). Lower surfaces are painted in RLM 76 (*Lichtblau*).

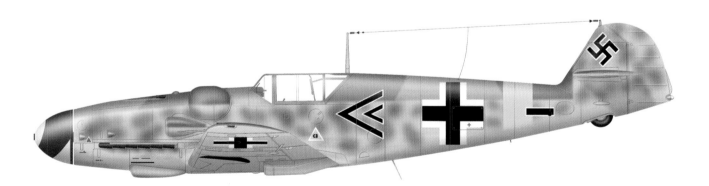

Messerschmitt Bf 109G-6, II./JG52, 1943

This fighter received standard factory camouflage of RLM 74 (*Dunkelgrau, grünlich*)/RLM 75 (*Mittelgrau*) on upper surfaces with blotches of RLM 70 (*Schwarzgrün*) and RLM 02 (RLM *Grau*). Lower surfaces are painted in RLM 76 (*Lichtblau*).

Colour views by Andrey Yurgenson

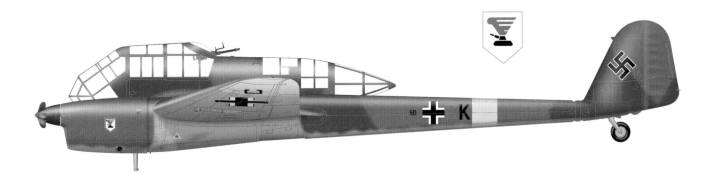

Focke Wulf Fw 189A-1, 2./(H)31

This aircraft is camouflaged in the colours of the early stage of the war (1939–40): upper surfaces are painted in RLM 70 (*Schwarzgrün*) and RLM 71 (*Dunkelgrün*), and the lower surfaces are painted in RLM 65 (*Hellbrau* of 1941 standard). The squadron badge is painted on the outer sides of the engine nacelles.

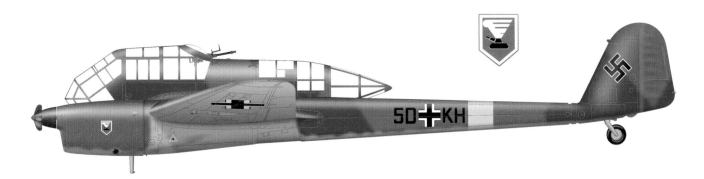

Focke Wulf Fw 189A-1, 2./(H)31

The aircraft is camouflaged in the colours of the early stage of the war (1939–40): upper surfaces are painted in RLM 70 (*Schwarzgrün*) and RLM 71 (*Dunkelgrün*), and the lower surfaces are painted in RLM 65 (*Hellbrau* of 1941 standard). The squadron badge is painted on the outer sides of the engine nacelles.

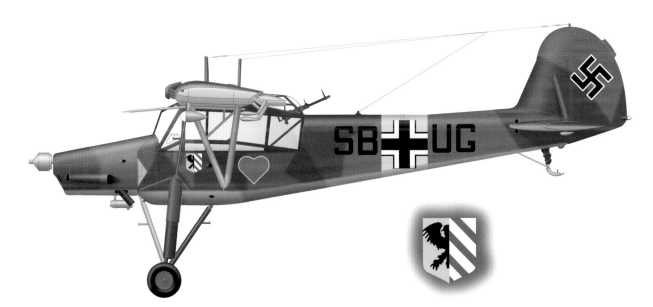

Fiesler Fi 156C-1, I./JG54 *Grünher*

This aircraft is camouflaged in the colours of the early stage of the war (1939–40): upper surfaces are painted in RLM 70 (*Schwarzgrün*) and RLM 71 (*Dunkelgrün*), and the lower surfaces are painted in RLM 65 (*Hellbrau* of 1941 standard). The squadron badge is painted under the cockpit.

Colour views by Andrey Yurgenson

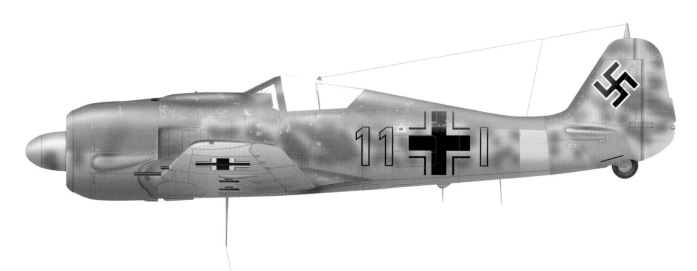

Focke Wulf Fw 190A-3, JG51, Orel, 1943

Early version of the aircraft camouflage scheme. The upper surfaces are painted in RLM 74 (*Dunkelgrau, grünlich*)/RLM 75 (*Mittelgrau*), and lower – in RLM 76 (*Lichtblau*).

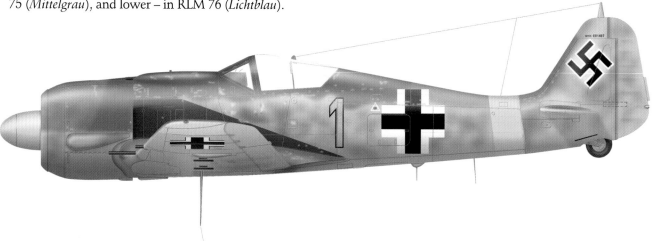

Focke Wulf Fw 190A-4 'Yellow 1', III./JG51, Orel, 1943

Flown by *Unteroffizier* Herbert Bareuther. Early version of the aircraft camouflage scheme. The upper surfaces are painted in RLM 74 (*Dunkelgrau, grünlich*)/RLM 75 (*Mittelgrau*), and lower – in RLM 76 (*Lichtblau*).

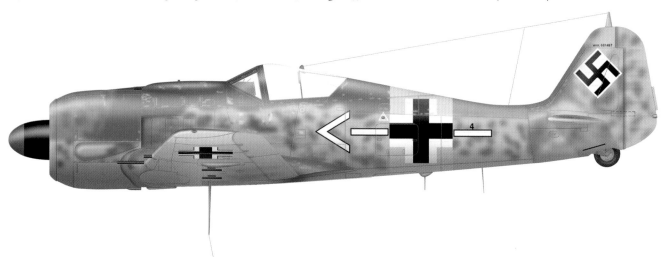

Focke Wulf Fw 190A-4, JG54, Krasnogvardeysk, 1943

Flown by the *Kommodore* of JG54 Hubertus Von Bonin. Early version of the aircraft camouflage scheme. The upper surfaces are painted in RLM 74 (*Dunkelgrau, grünlich*)/RLM 75 (*Mittelgrau*), and lower – in RLM 76 (*Lichtblau*).

Colour views by Andrey Yurgenson

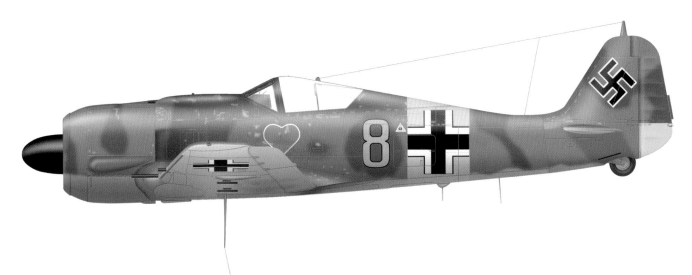

Focke Wulf Fw 190A-5 'Yellow 8', III./JG54, Orel, 1943

Flown by *Staffelkapitän* Robert Weiss. The fighter wears a non-standard camouflage of shades of green. Lower surfaces – RLM 76 (*Lichtblau*). It is possible that this camouflage is applied over the standard combination of RLM 74/75/76.

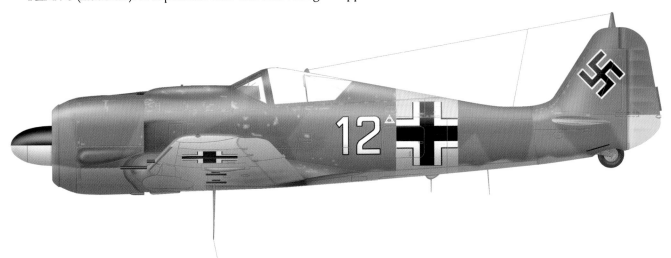

Focke Wulf Fw 190A-6 'White 12', I./JG54, 1943

Flown by *Staffelkapitän* Helmut Wettstein. The fighter wears a non-standard camouflage of shades pf green. Lower surfaces – RLM 76 (*Lichtblau*). It is possible that this camouflage is applied over the standard combination of RLM 74/75/76.

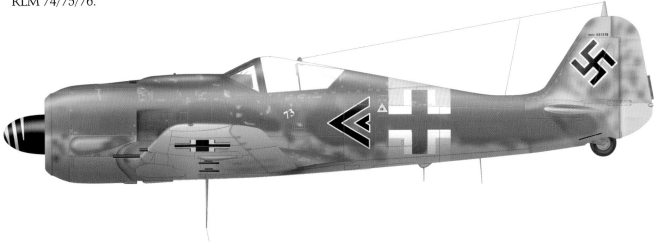

Focke Wulf Fw 190A-6, I./JG54, 1943

This camouflage in shades of green is possibly applied over the standard combination of RLM 74/75/76.

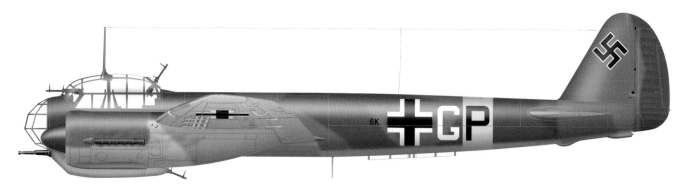

Junkers Ju 88A-14, 6/KG51, July 1943

The aircraft is camouflaged in the colours of the early stage of the war (1939–40): upper surfaces are painted in RLM 70 (*Schwarzgrün*) and RLM 71 (*Dunkelgrün*), and the lower surfaces are painted in RLM 65 (*Hellbrau* of 1941 standard).

Junkers Ju 87D-3, I./StG1, July 1943

The aircraft is camouflaged in the colours of the early stage of the war (1939–40): upper surfaces are painted in RLM 70 (*Schwarzgrün*) and RLM 71 (*Dunkelgrün*), and the lower surfaces are painted in RLM 65 (*Hellbrau* of 1941 standard).

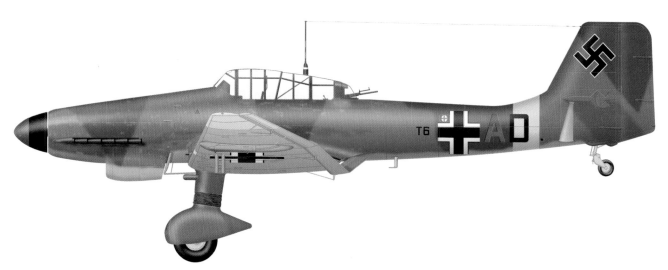

Junkers Ju 87D-3, II./StG1, July 1943

The aircraft is camouflaged in the colours of the early stage of the war (1939–40): upper surfaces are painted in RLM 70 (*Schwarzgrün*) and RLM 71 (*Dunkelgrün*), and the lower surfaces are painted in RLM 65 (*Hellbrau* of 1941 standard). Note red/black spinner.

Colour views by Andrey Yurgenson

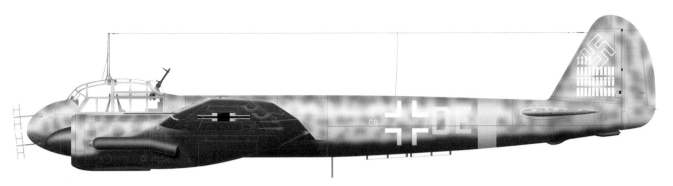

Junkers Ju 88C-6, IV./NJG5, 1943

Flown by *Hauptmann* H. zu Sain Wittgenstein. Night-type camouflage of this aircraft included RLM 76 (*Lichtblau*) with blotches of RLM 75 (*Mittelgrau*) on upper surfaces, and RLM 22 (*Schwarz*) on lower surfaces.

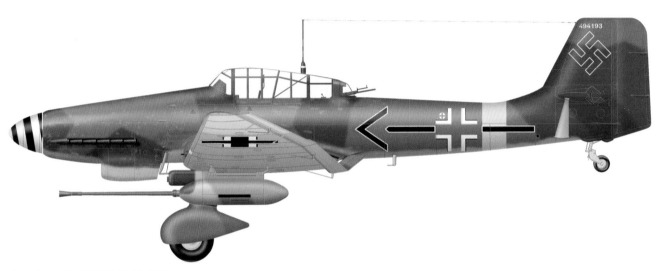

Junkers Ju 87G-2, StG2

The aircraft is camouflaged in the colours of the early stage of the war (1939–40): upper surfaces are painted in RLM 70 (*Schwarzgrün*) and RLM 71 (*Dunkelgrün*), and the lower surfaces are painted in RLM 65 (*Hellbrau* of 1941 standard). Note black spinner with white band.

Junkers Ju 87G-2, StG77

The aircraft is camouflaged in the colours of the early stage of the war (1939–40): upper surfaces are painted in RLM 70 (*Schwarzgrün*) and RLM 71 (*Dunkelgrün*), and the lower surfaces are painted in RLM 65 (*Hellbrau* of 1941 standard). Note black/white spinner. Yellow bands on the fuselage and wingtips were a characteristic feature of all *Luftwaffe* aircraft on the Eastern Front of this period of the war.

Colour views by Andrey Yurgenson

↻ Soviet officers examine the wrecks of a shot-down Ju 52 transport.

distribution of efforts between aviation and artillery. It was also decided to fight the enemy in different areas and altitudes and to locate attack aircraft and their fighter-cover units at the same or close-by airfields. In order to get the aviation control closer to the battlefield, additional command posts were also established and positioned in the direction of the main strikes by ground forces, some 7–8km from the front line. Additional airstrips were also prepared and it should be noted that preparation of these joint actions by the aviation and ground troops were similar to those made by Germans in summer 1941. The actions given to false concentration of forces played their role as well and as a result, the enemy supposed that the main strike would be made by the Soviet forces on the right wing of the Voronezh Front, in the Sumy direction.

Success of the Soviet counter-offensive

On the night of August 3 the German troops and their 'footholds' were attacked by Li-2 and Il-4 night bombers from the 6th Air Corps as well as by the U-2 light bombers from the 208th NBAD of the 2nd Air Army. The aviation and artillery preparation started two hours before the main attack, and about 6,000 guns and 500 attack aircraft participated. The 5th Air Army concentrated its bombers in a groups of 50–100 Pe-2 planes each (division groups were lead by Colonels I.S. Polbin, F.I. Dobysh, and G.V. Gribakin), and attacked the

◐ The navigator of an He 111 in flight.

◐ Soviet technicians remove the photo camera from a Pe-2 reconnaissance aircraft after the mission.

◑ The ground crew of StG2 bring in the bombs for loading the Ju 87 dive bombers. Note the SC 250 and SC 70 bombs in the foreground.

◐ *Luftwaffe* officers receive the latest information about the battle situation from the tank crews.

♠ Senior Lieutenant I.E. Komarov exchanges the experience of his latest combat sortie with his commander and comrades.

♠ Commander of the Voronesh Front, Army General N.F. Vatutin (to the right), and a member of the Military Council N.S. Khrushchev watch the air battle.

♠ A navigator of one of the German bombers is photographing the target.

♠ A group of La-5 fighters in air patrol over the front line.

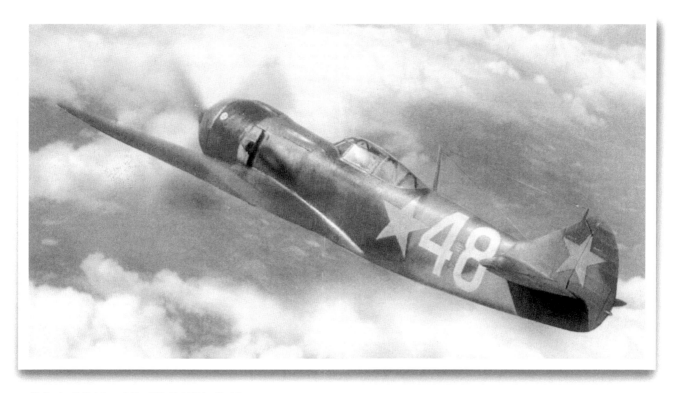

ↂ An La-5 fighter of the 8th GvIAD in flight.

main points of resistance of the first line of the German defence, and the 2nd Air Army attacked in echelons, using small groups of 6–12 aircraft, on the targets in the second line of the defence.

Using this advantage, the Soviet troops entered the German defence line by some 5–7km and as a result, there created the prerequisites for pulling the 1st and 5th Tank Armies into the battle. Under the order of General S.A. Krasovsky, the 202nd BAD made two concentrated strikes – with forty-three Pe-2s (from 12.10 till 12.23 hours) and by sixty-three Pe-2 bombers (from 18.00 till 18.20 hours), which stopped the Germans bringing up their reserves. Especially effective was the strike of the Petlyakov bombers on the artillery and anti-aircraft batteries to the north-west of Belgorod. The same high accuracy was demonstrated by the units of the 291st ShAD and 5th ShAK. In the meantime the Soviet fighters maintained air superiority over the battlefield, not allowing the enemy planes to slow the ground troops' offensive.

The Soviet tank armies took the opportunity to exploit the success. General N.K. Popel recollected: "During three hours our artillery batteries and bombers loosened the ground, mixed it with pieces of concrete blocks, logs, iron core, and the bodies of enemy soldiers. In the meantime our tanks got to the very front line... Probably only the tank crews like M.E. Katukov, and A.L. Getman who were there at the start of the combat in summer 1941 will understand the feelings which seized me, and in this moment we stood straight in the trench and eagerly watched the T-34 tanks overtaking each other, the squadrons of the lightning-like attack

aircraft and the bombers spreading their wings in the skies above us." During the first day of the counter-offensive the pilots of the 2nd and 5th Air Armies carried out 2,671 combat sorties, which were countered by only 569 Luftwaffe flights. The Germans claimed fifty-six Soviet planes, with thirty accredited to the hunter aces of III./JG52. They achieved most success by surprise attacks and lost only one pilot – the experienced Oberleutnant R. Trepte, most likely shot down by the fighters from the groups of Captain V.N. Orlov or Lieutenant S.D. Gorelov of the 13th IAP. This regiment carried out five sorties and for the first time utilised the newer La-5FN fighters along with the standard La-5s. The same high activity was demonstrated by the pilots of the 236th and 437th IAP, and according to the crew reports, in fifteen air engagements they shot down twelve Bf 109s.

Several air strikes by Junkers of I./KG3 on the columns of Soviet troops in the Yakovlevo region were carried out in the second half of August 3 but they were unable to slow the offensive. However, on the next day 8th Air Corps units increased their efforts and the German aviators responded with 1,119 day sorties. On August 4 large groups of Ju 87 dive bombers made multiple strikes on the ground troops; the appearance of these dive bombers was preceded by 'cleaning' the region from Soviet fighters using patrols of Bf 109s, while the pathfinder aircraft dropped coloured smoke bombs. The air engagements now became longer and more intense and according to Soviet pilots, the enemy Bf 109 pilots feigned exit from an air engagement by diving, but then gained altitude in a combat turn and

() Fighter pilots watch the landing of attack aircraft.

() According to a daily report of the Soviet information office, Junior Lieutenant A.V. Nikolaev evacuated his comrade from the 88th GvIAP from the hatch of his La-5 after his emergency landing. Both pilots successfully arrived at Ivnya airfield (80 km to the south of Kursk).

() Commander of the 290th ShAD General I.P. Mironenko talks to pilots.

() A German armoured car Sd.Kfz.251 destroyed by armour-piercing bombs.

rejoined the fight. In another other case, a four-aircraft formation of German fighters, noting the concentration of Soviet fighters at high altitude, carried out swift attacks from the rear, shooting down four Il-2s and three La-5s.

On 4 August, JG52 was active against the Soviet units and the combat record of the 8th Air Corps indicated that the bombers carried out the most powerful strikes to the north of Tomarovka, while dive bombers and attack aircraft operated to the south-east of the village, concentrating their efforts on the destruction of Soviet tanks. It was also noted in Soviet documents that the greatest damage was inflicted on the units of the 3rd Mechanised Corps of the 1st Tank Army, which still managed to make a noticeable advance compared to its neighboring 6th and 29th Tank Corps. Nevertheless, it should be stated that both sides considerably exaggerated their successes, especially the results of their bomb strikes on tanks and other armoured targets. For a more intensive use of aviation,

the command of the 8th Air Corps positioned some of its units, including fighter, attack and anti-tank aircraft to some of the most advanced airstrips, especially those close to the front line. However, by doing this, the Germans fell under heavy attack by Soviet tanks and infantry and when retreating, they were forced to blow-up several Fw 190s, Hs 129s, 46s and Ju 87s.

By now the Germans had retreated a considerable part of their forces to the south and south-west, primarily from Belgorod to Kharkov and further out to Poltava, and Grayvoron to Akhtyrka. Some of the retreating columns included hundreds of trucks with several tanks among them, and one such column was spotted by the reconnaissance planes of the 511th Reconnaissance Air Regiment, and all the bomb and attack units of two armies were immediately sent to strike and the aviators of the 5th Air Army added thirty-five tanks and 150 trucks into their records. The Soviet bombers continued their raids on Bogodukhov and Trostyanets railway stations, where they destroyed several trains, and attack aircraft provided air cover for the tank armies. Marshal G.K. Zhukov presented the 'Commander Rumyantsev' plan which was approved by Stalin on the night of August 7 and at the same time the advance on Kharkov was authorized, and Soviet troops would continue their combat at Donbass after an operational pause. The military councils of the South and South-Western Fronts received the order to be ready for an offensive on 13–14 August and by that time the two tank armies, which had been introduced into the battle, would have approached the towns of Valki and Merefa, and crossed the roads from Kharkov-Poltava and Kharkov-Krasnodar, so cutting in two the main forces of the Army Group 'South'.

Hitler and his generals obviously didn't expect such a sweeping onset of the Soviet troops, as they had supposed that the Red Army was extremely weakened. When assessing the intents of the Red Army command, the German intelligence noted just a day before the Soviet counter-offensive that "The intelligence data of the Army Group 'South' for the last days shows that the large groups of forces started to move to the region to the south and south-west of Kursk. This offensive, which is expected to start in about two weeks, will be in the directions – on the right flank to the 7th Corps of the 2nd Army, and on the left flank to the north of Kharkov, and will have the goal of making a powerful strike on the depth of the right flank of Army Group 'South'.' (Thus, the Germans incorrectly defined not only the time but the also the location of the planned strike). In the following days, the 8th Air Corps carried out no less than 1,000 daily sorties and attempting to slow down the offensive, the German aircraft bombing troop columns, water crossings, and the control and communication posts. In the course of one such raid, a Ju 88 hit the command post of the 5th Attack Air Corps, and the Deputy Commander of the Voronezh Front, Army General I.R. Apanasenko was mortally wounded. Up to 100 Ju 87s and fifty Ju 88s and He 111s participated in some of the most concentrated air strikes and managed to slow down the Soviet tanks allowing the combat groups of the 11th and 19th Tank Divisions as well as 255th and 352nd Rifle Divisions to avoid defeat and to keep control over the highly important road from Grayvoron to Akhtyrka.

In some cases the Soviet fighters spoiled the German attacks by selfless actions. On 7 August a six-Yak-1 formation of the 236th IAP of the 201st IAD (leader – Junior Lieutenant Yumkin) attacked four He 111 bombers in the vicinity of Mikoyanovka. The bombers flew without air cover and tried to hide in the clouds. Senior Sergeant Piskunov persistently followed one of the bombers, used up all his ammunition, and then ram attacked the enemy. The damaged fighter

↺ Major D.L. Lomovtsev thanks Lieutenant Garin for his exceptional performance on a combat mission.

∩ A pair of early series La-5s of the 302nd IAD at an unprepared airfield to the south of Kursk.

∩ The crew of a 20-mm gun of the 7th German motorized anti-aircraft artillery regiment cover a crossing of the Severny Donets river.

∩ A technician of the Shurashov Wing checks the readiness of a Pe-2 for the next sortie after repairs done by technician Vikhlyaev, 293rd BAD of the 1st BAK.

∩ Heinkel of *Oberleutnant* Ludwig Havighorst of KG27 on a combat mission.

then made an emergency landing at the field. Commander of III./KG27 *Hauptmann* K. Mayer was seriously wounded in this air combat, but managed to return to Kharkov-Voytchenko. The situation continued to be quite difficult for the Germans. On August 8 the Commander of NAGr6 *Major* H. Rinke reported to headquarters that the Russians brought about 200 tanks into the breakthrough area, creating a gap between the troops of the 4th Air Army and *Kampfgruppe Kempf*. When analysing the situation, the OKW stated on the same day that 'The enemy managed to expand the gap considerably by strong tank attacks. Its advanced units are about 40 km to the north-west of Kharkov'.

Assessing the activity of Soviet aviation from 3 till 8 August, Marshal G.K. Zhukov noted in his report to Stalin that the total number of day and night sorties was more than 13,000, of which 60% were aimed at elimination of troops and equipment. At the same time, an active fight for air superiority took place – and in 300 air engagements about 400 German aircraft were shot down or damaged, while the losses of the Soviet side were 200. 'Captives confirmed the exceptional effectiveness of our aviation in this operation', noted Zhukov. This was also confirmed by the natives in the liberated territories'. According to the Marshal's opinion, Soviet aviation supported the breakthrough in the enemy's defence line, covered the entrance of the tank armies in the breakthrough area, and assisted in the growth of tactical success. Among the main shortcomings Zhukov noted insufficient organization of air reconnaissance, poor cooperation between different types of aviation, and intolerable cases of bombing friendly troops in a fast-changing situation.

Germans increase their opposition

In the face of solid Soviet air supremacy it was decided to strengthen the *Luftwaffe* units which were part of the 8th Air Corps in the shortest possible time. During

↷ The pilots of 270th IAP pose near a Yak-1 fighter.

↺ A German communication post arranged under the wing of a shot-down Il-2.

↷ Commander of the 800th ShAP Major A.I. Mitrofanov.

↷ Deputy squadron commander of the 820th IAP S.D. Podshivalnikov many times led attack aircraft formations into combat. A photo from 1944.

➲ Attack aircraft pilot Junior Lieutenant S.V. Miloshenkov selflessly fought near Belgorod and Kharkov.

↷ The pilots of II./JG3 discuss the events of an air engagement.

◑ German tank crews before a counter-attack watch a strike of Luftwaffe dive bombers.

◑ A German SS tank crew watch the air battle.

◑ Comrades of the 41st IAP congratulate Senior Lieutenant A.G. Pavlov with a victory.

◑ A group of attack aircraft takes off for the next sortie.

7–10 August no fewer than eight air groups (I./JG51 and IV./JG51, I./JG54, III./StG3, II./KG3, III./KG4, II./KG27 and III./KG51) with some 270–280 aircraft were relocated from the 6th Air Fleet to the area of Poltava, Kirovograd, Mirgorod, Dnepropetrovsk and Zaporoshye. The bombers of the 4th Air Corps of the 4th Air Fleet, which had been active in the Soviet South and South-Western Fronts, were also transferred. At least 170 arrived at the main German air base at Poltava on the morning of 10 August and others were parked at the Bolshaya Rudra airfield to the north of the town. The Germans carried out a counter-strike in the region of Akhtyrka, which they began on August 18 facilitated by the regrouping and relocation of forces from Bryansk. At that time the Germans concentrated up to 200 tanks in the narrow parts of the front and crushed the left flank of the Soviet 27th Army with the intensive support of the *Luftwaffe*. The German tanks and motorised infantry units were to be stopped at all costs.

The combat actions record book of the OKW noted that by August 24 'in the region to the south of Akhtyrka were the remains of 299 encircled enemy

tanks. 188 guns were captured, and 1,800 men were taken prisoner.' Heavy battles near Akhtyrka caused concern for the Commander-in-Chief Headquarters and 'The events of the last days showed', noted Stalin to General N.F. Vatutin, – 'that you did not take into account the experience of earlier combat [meaning the cut-away striking group of the Voronezh Front in February 1943 – author's note] and continue to repeat the old mistakes, both during the planning stage, as well as during the performance of the operation. The desire for offensive far and wide, and for capturing the maximum possible area of territory without securing the success and strong support of the flanks of the striking groups... lead to the dissipation of resources, and allowed the enemy to perform counter-strikes to the flanks and rear of our groupings, which had advanced considerably, and which were not supported by other groups. As a result of these actions by the enemy our troops suffered considerable and unsustainable losses. We also lost an advantageous position for destruction of the Kharkov grouping of the enemy.' The Commander of one of the motorised corps, Colonel A.Kh. Babadjanyan, also noted the following about the battles where hundreds of Soviet and German tanks clashed in the narrow strips at the front: 'aviation provided poor support to our combat units and at the critical moments our tank units carried the main burden of combat against large enemy forces, who had the full support of German aircraft'.

Multiple air engagements spread over the battle area, and no side achieved air superiority as the situation changed quickly. The squadron commander of the 728th IAP of 256th IAD, Captain A.V. Vorozheikin remembered one such dogfight which took place over Tomarovka to the west of Belgorod: 'I just managed to rush out of the ball of fire and smoke, and immediately spotted the German fighter nearby. I quickly approached and fired a burst with my cannon. The enemy dashed aside, I followed him. My second burst was followed by another and I saw the hits, but felt that I hurried – it was not a deadly fire. I tried to aim again, but more precisely, but couldn't – the Messerschmitt started to make wide rolls and I couldn't get him into the crosshairs of my gunsight. Of course I could try to catch him in such manoeuvres, but I should not be carried away. Being concerned about another enemy pair, I dropped the agile Messerschmitt, and looked around for another target …'.

However, most of Soviet pilots were poorly trained and many of them undertook their first combat engagements with the enemy in August 1943 and this was possibly the main reason for the many German successes in the air. The German pilots had 'mastered' their aircraft and used the strengths of their steeds – Messerschmitts fought in the vertical, while the Focke-Wulfs attacked from dives and did not avoid head-on attacks. Among the most effective 'hunters', were *Oberleutnant* W. Nowotny of I./JG54 and the pilots of III./JG52: *Oberleutnant* W. Krupinski, *Leutnants* B. Korts, F. Obleser and E. Hartmann and the Commander of the group III./JG52, *Hauptmann* G. Rall scored his 175th victory on the evening of August 7 to the west of Belgorod.

During the hot days of August

At the same time, in other areas of the front, the Soviet troops kept moving further to the west and south-west and in the course of the offensive, the aviation units operated from several advanced locations and captured airfields. However, the rear units were still far behind the advancing troops, but the supply units could not manage to deliver the ammunition and food in time, as well as to arrange the advance air strips. When retreating, the Germans were destroying the railway lines and stations, so a lot of time was required for their

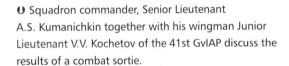

↺ Squadron commander, Senior Lieutenant A.S. Kumanichkin together with his wingman Junior Lieutenant V.V. Kochetov of the 41st GvIAP discuss the results of a combat sortie.

↺ Commander of the 240th IAP, HSU Lieutenant Colonel S.I. Podorozhny, of the 41st GvIAP discuss the results of a combat sortie.

↺ Lieutenant General V.G. Ryazanov commanded the most famous Soviet attack aircraft unit – the 1st ShAK.

↺ Commander of SchG1 *Major* Alfred Druschel carried out about 900 combat sorties by the end of the battle at the Orel-Kursk salient.

restoration. The above factors had an effect on the Soviet aviation. At the end of the offensive, the 202nd BAD, still based in Stariy Oskol, operating almost at the limit of their Pe-2s and many aircraft were forced to make intermediate landings at the fighter unit airfields due to a shortage of fuel.

At the height of the offensive, many commanders were also highly critical of fighter pilots, especially of the fighter units. This was not only due to the short time of air cover. For instance, the Commander of the 40th Army, General K.S. Moskalenko mentioned, as a typical case, the events which took place about noon of August 14. According to his observation, six La-5s spotted two Bf 109s, but instead of engaging the enemy the Soviet pilots called for the support of four more La-5s. Then, when they eventually attacked, the Soviet fighters did not spot fifteen Ju 88s, which on his opinion were hard to miss, and the results of their raid were clearly visible. Expressing his indignation to General S.A. Krasovskiy about such actions of the fighters, General K.S. Moskalenko concluded: 'This example spoiled the impression of the huge and effective work which has been done by the units of the 2nd Air Army in the course of the operation. In our section of the operations, not one bombing mission was lost, and no enemy plane shot down, but so far, our fighter pilots are still not being used to seek out the enemy in combat, and to impose themselves. At the same time the actions of the attack aircraft and bombers are admired by the soldiers and commanders. Our planes approach the target in organised formations, and carry out selfless strikes. However, the old shortcoming still remain – our aircraft stay over the target for too short a time and make only one bomb run. General N.P. Kamanin also noted: 'What a misfortune it was – our fighter cover was small, while the leader of the attack aircraft did not spot the threat, lost the moment and … eleven of our planes fell to the ground one after the other, a heavy and bloody lesson'.

The units of the 8th Air Corps carried out 758

⋒ Young pilots of the 240th IAP (left to right) – Yu. Lobenok, A. Amelin, and K. Evstigneev at Urazovo airfield.

⋓ A meeting of the members of the Young Communist League at one of the units of the 1st ShAK.

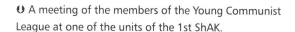

⋒ One of the multiple aircraft mock-ups which were set up by the Germans along an airfield boundary in order to protect aircraft from bomb strikes.

⋒ Combat damage to a Pe-2 wing.

⋔ A Ju 87D dive bomber shot down in an air battle to the north of Kharkov.

⋔ One of the first Bf 109G-6s, which arrived with I./JG52 in the course of the battle.

⋔ The ground crew prepares the aircraft of the Commander of the 617th ShAP Major D.L. Lomovtsev for the next combat mission.

⋔ Senior Lieutenant V.K. Kuleshov (to the right) of the 41st GvIAP together with his wingman near an La-5.

sorties on August 19 and 1,018 sorties the following day. According to the KG27 combat record book, in the course of the intensive combat work, extraordinary situations arose quite often. For instance, after two raids from Uman airfield, the unit had no more bombs left. Then the *Geschwaderkommodore* von Beust ordered them to load air mines into the bomb bays of their Heinkels. Commander of the German 11th Corps *General* Erhard Raus, who saw this evening bomb raid, recalled: 'Fountains of earth were raised to the sky, accompanied by terrible thunder and shakes, which resembled earthquakes... Wing after wing, the bombers freely approached the bombing point and shortly all the villages where the Soviet tanks were stationed were on fire. The sea of dust and clouds of smoke, highlighted by the sunset, brightly contrasted with the black mushrooms of smoke from the burning tanks – the victims of our air raid. A horrible picture of death and destruction!' After such a powerful strike, the Russians were forced to drop their offensive plan, even in spite of Stalin's order.

During 19 and 20 August German bombers provided the main support to the SS *Panzergrenadier Division Totenkopf* which participated in the counter-strike near Akhtyrka. In the air raid the German aircraft destroyed twenty-four tanks, two armoured trains, and more than 150 trucks and armoured vehicles. Nevertheless the Germans were forced to stop their actions and retreat. Now the units of the Stepnoy Front carried out fierce fighting on the approaches to Kharkov, trying to encircle the enemy. The Kharkov-Poltave road, which was still in German hands, was heavily and continuously bombed by the 5th Air Army, and on 21 and 22 August alone more than 1,300 combat sorties were flown, in which Soviet aviation destroyed fifty-seven tanks, 291 trucks, up to 130 guns, and about 1,000 soldiers and officers were scattered. On the night of August 23 Kharkov was completely liberated from the Germans.

↻ Lieutenant A.I. Mayorov of the 2nd GvIAP gets out of a Lavochkin cockpit. During the battle he scored eight personal victories and two victories in a group. On 7 August 1943, in course of a combat mission over Khotinets, he shot down an Fw 189 and Ju 87, after which he was awarded with a star of HSU.

Chapter 8

Outcome of the Kursk battle

With all the different coverage and appraisal of events which took place in summer 1943 in the Kursk area, Soviet and Western historians are united in their assertion that this was one of the biggest battles of the Second World War. According to Marshal G.K. Zhukov: 'In this battle, not only the select and most powerful German troops were overwhelmed, but also the trust of the German army and people in Hitler's Nazi leadership was irrevocably lost, as well as their belief in Germany's capability of opposing the increasing power of the Soviet Union. The defeat of the main group of German forces in the Kursk area prepared the ground for the further wide offensive operations of the Soviet forces...' *Generalfeldmarschall*

Erich von Manstein admitted that Operation 'Zitadelle' was the last attempt to retain our initiative.

When the operation ended in failure, the initiative finally passed to the Soviet side. In this respect Operation 'Zitadelle' was the decisive, turning point in the war on the Eastern Front. His position was echoed by the well-known German historian P. Carell who said, 'In the same way as Waterloo determined the fate of Napoleon in 1815, putting an end to his governing and changing the look of Europe, the Russian victory at Kursk was the turning point of the war and led directly to the collapse of Hitler and defeat of Germany in two years, thus changing the look of the whole world'. While the global appraisal of the battle is clear, discussions over the application of different types of forces, their cooperation, and corresponding losses are still active. The assessment

↻ Junior Lieutenant V.A. Tarelkin in the cockpit of an Il-2. 22 July 1943.

of the opposition of the Red Army Air Force and the *Luftwaffe* near Kursk is still not finalised. There is an opinion in the West that the units of the 4th and 6th Air Fleets inflicted heavy losses on the enemy in the air and on the ground, while their own losses were minimal. The opinion of the Soviet side is clear from a statement of the Commander of the 2nd Air Army: 'The Soviet Air Force successfully and fully resolved the whole complex set of tasks given to them, starting with reaching superiority in the air, up to and including participation in the pursuit of the defeated enemy's forces and fighting with its reserves. From that angle the Kursk battle was the most important stage in the development of tactical warfare by Soviet aviation'.

In the course of repelling the German offensive in Operation 'Zitadelle', the Red Army Air Force lost about 1,000 aircraft while the *Luftwaffe* losses in the same period approached 400, while 270–280 more planes required repair. When supporting the Soviet offensive in Operation 'Kutuzov', Soviet aviation lost 1,000 more aircraft, while 550 more were lost during Operation 'Commander Rumyantsev'. The heaviest losses were suffered by the 15th Air Army (from 12 July till 13 August its losses were 559 aircraft, or seventeen aircraft per day) and the 2nd Air Army (from 3 till 23 August the losses were 341 aircraft, or 15.5 planes per day). The total number of aircraft lost, including Long-Range Aviation and Air Defence, was 2,800 planes, and according to records of the Luftwaffe for July and August 1943, 1,463 aircraft of the 4th and 6th Air Fleets were written off, while 1,000 more had been damaged with 469 needing repair. The losses of German aviation in the Kursk battle could be assessed as 2,000 aircraft destroyed or damaged, as the 4th Air Fleet was also operating at that time in the

⋒⋓ Ambulance aviation evacuate wounded.

⋒ German radio operators in action.

◑ Senior Lieutenant I. N. Alishkin was one of the best pilots of the 617th ShAP in the battles near Belgorod and Kharkov, and carried out 27 combat sorties from 5 July till 23 August 1943, destroyed 7 tanks, 13 trucks, and exploded two ammunition stores.

◑ Captain S. Zharikov near Il-2 c/n 1876643 clarifies the route of the forthcoming mission.

◑ Among the new Soviet fighter types which were used for the first time in the Kursk battle, the important role was played by the Yak-9D fighter with increased fuel capacity.

Donbass area, the Black Sea, and in other locations.

The most frequent mistake made was Soviet fighters acting in relatively large groups of twelve to eighteen aircraft, readily entering air engagements with pairs or four-aircraft formations of Focke-Wulfs or Messerschmitts, so allowing them to tie up the Soviet fighters and drag them from their patrol area, allowing formations of bombers to continue unhindered. A specific feature of the Kursk battle was also the fact that Red Army Air Force commander Marshal A.A. Novikov and the Chief of the *Luftwaffe* General Headquarters *Generaloberst* Hans Jeschonnek personally commanded the aviation activities. Novikov and his deputies, Generals S.A. Khudyakov and G.A. Vorozheykin participated in the development of the Air Force's plan for combat actions in the defensive and offensive part of the operation, coordinated the cooperation of the air armies and ground troops, correlated the flights of the Air Armies and Long-Range Aviation, and gave orders to the reserve units of the Commander-in-Chief's Headquarters. However, they did not manage to reach close cooperation with the neighboring air armies – each of the armies acted strictly within the borders of their corresponding fronts.

Generaloberst Hans Jeschonnek was also resolving crucial tasks – he was coordinating the actions of the 4th and 6th Air Fleets, and commanding the relocation of units from one grouping to the other. In spite of separate multiple successes (for example in the destruction of a large number of Soviet tanks or planes at one time), the main goal of the operation, as it was understood by the Chief of General Headquarters, was not reached. The strength of Soviet forces was increasing, and the weakening of the German ground forces forced *Luftwaffe* to disperse their available resources to many parts of the front. The situation was aggravated by the continuous intrigues of *Reichsmarschall* Göring, while the successful destructive air raid of about 600 British bombers on the test range in Peenemünde gave the final blow to Jeschonnek – and as he could not find a way out of this critical situation, he shot himself on August 19 1943.

Appendix I – Combat Strengths

★ Combat strength of the Soviet 2nd Air Army – beginning of July 1943

Unit	Commander	Aircraft Type
4th IAK	Major General I.D. Podgorny	
294th IAD	Colonel V.V. Sukhoryabov	Yak-1, Yak-7
302nd IAD	Colonel B.I. Litvinov	La-5
5th IAK	Major General D.P. Galunov	
205th IAD	Colonel Yu.A. Nemtsovich	Yak-1, Yak-7
8th GvIAD	Colonel I.P. Laryushkin	La-5
1st BAK	Colonel I.S. Polbin	
1st GvBAD	Colonel F.I. Dobysh	Pe-2
293rd BAD	Colonel G.V. Gribakin	Pe-2
1st ShAK	Lieutenant General V.G. Ryazanov	
266th ShAD	Colonel F.G. Rodyakin	Il-2
292nd ShAD	Major General F.A. Agaltsov	Il-2
203rd IAD	Major General K.G. Baranchuk	Yak-1
291st ShAD	Major General A.N. Vitruk	Il-2
208th NBAD	Colonel L.N. Yuzeev	U-2, R-5
454th BAP	Major A.A. Tatulov	A-20B
50th KRAP	Lieutenant Colonel I.Ya. Mironov	Pe-2

Note: In the course of the defence operations, the 205th IAD was moved to the rear, whilst the 256th IAD under the leadership of Colonel N.S. Gerasimov, and flying the Yak-7 and Yak-9, was introduced to the 5th IAK.

★ Combat strength of the Soviet 17th Air Army – beginning of July 1943

Unit	Commander	Aircraft Type
1st SAK	Major General V.I. Shevchenko	
288th IAD	Colonel B.A. Smirnov	Yak-1
5th GvShAD	Colonel L.V. Kolomeytsev	Il-2
3rd SAK	Major General V.I. Aladinsky	
207th IAD	Colonel A.P. Osadchy	La-5, Yak-1
290th ShAD	Major General P.I. Mironenko	Il-2
9th SAK	Major General O.V. Tolstikov	
295th IAD	Colonel N.F. Balanov	La-5
305th ShAD	Lieutenant Colonel N.G. Mikhevichev	Il-2
306th ShAD	Colonel A.F. Isupov	Il-2
244th BAD	Major General V.I. Klevtsov	A-20B
262nd NBAD	Colonel G.I. Belitsky	U-2

★

★ Combat strength of the Soviet 16th Air Army – beginning of July 1943

Unit	Commander	Aircraft Type
6th IAK	Major General A.B. Yumashev	
273rd IAD	Colonel I.E. Fedorov	Yak-1, Yak-7, Yak-9
2279th IAD	Colonel F.N. Dementiev	La-5
6th SAK	Major General I.D. Antoshkin	
221st BAD	Colonel S.F. Buzylev	A-20B, Boston III
282nd IAD	Colonel A.M. Ryazanov	Yak-1
3rd BAK	Major General A.Z. Karavatsky	
241st BAD	Colonel I.G. Kurylenko	Pe-2
301st BAD	Colonel F.M. Fedorenko	Pe-2
1st GvIAD	Lieutenant Colonel I.V. Krupenin	Yak-1, P-39
283rd IAD	Colonel S.P. Denisov	Yak-1, Yak-7
286th IAD	Colonel I.I. Ivanov	Yak-1, La-5
2nd GvShAD	Colonel G.I. Komarov	Il-2
299th ShAD	Colonel I.V. Krupsky	Il-2
271st NBAD	Lieutenant Colonel K.P. Rasskazov	U-2
16th ODRAP	Major D.S. Sherstyuk	A-20B, Pe-2
98th GvODRAP	Lieutenant Colonel B.P. Artemyev	Pe-2

✠ Combat strength of the 1st German Air Division – beginning of July 1943

Unit	Commander	Aircraft Type
NAGr4	Major T. Vinek	Bf 109G, Bf 110
NAGr10	Oberleutnant W. Stein	Hs 126B, Fw 189A
NAGr15	Major H. Correns	Fw 189A
StG1	Oberstleutnant G. Pressler	Ju 87D
I./StG1	Major H. Kaubisch	Ju 87D
II./StG1	Major O. Ernst	Ju 87D
III./StG1	Hauptman F. Lang	Ju 87D
III./StG3	Hauptman E. Jacob	Ju 87D
ZG1	Oberstleutnant J. Blechschmidt	Bf 110G
I./ZG1	Hauptman W. Hermann	Bf 110E, Bf 110F, Bf 110G
KG51	Major H. Heise	Ju 88A
II./KG51	Major H. Voss	Ju 88A
III./KG51	Hauptman W. Rath	Ju 88A, Ju 88C
III./KG1	Hauptman W. Kanther	Ju 88A, Ju 88C
KG4	Oberstleutnant W. Klosinski	He 111H
II./KG4	Major R. Graubner	He 111H
III./KG4	Major K. Neumann	He 111H
KG53	Oberstleutnant F. Pockrandt	He 111H
I./KG53	Major K. Rauer	He 111H
III./KG53	Major E. Allmendinger	He 111H
JG51	Oberstleutnant K.G. Nordmann	Fw 190A
I./JG51	Major E. Leie	Fw 190A
III./JG51	Hauptman F. Losigkeit	Fw 190A
IV./JG51	Major R. Resch	Fw 190A
I./JG54	Hauptman R. Seiler	Fw 190A

✠ Combat strength of the 8th German Air Corps – beginning of July 1943

Unit	Commander	Aircraft Type
NAGr6	*Hauptman* W. Sell	Bf 109G, Bf 110G, Hs 126B, Fw 189A
StG2	*Major* E. Kupfer	Ju 87D
I./StG2	*Hauptman* B. Dilley	Ju 87D
II./StG2	*Hauptman* H.-K. Stepp	Ju 87D, Ju 87G
III./StG2	*Hauptman* W. Krauss	Ju 87D
StG77	*Major* H. Bruck	Ju 87D
I./StG77	*Hauptman* W. Roell	Ju 87D
II./StG77	*Hauptman* H. Leicht	Ju 87D
III./StG77	*Major* F. Kieslich	Ju 87D
SchG1	*Major* A. Druschel	Bf 110G
I./SchG1	*Hauptman* G. Dörffel	Fw 190A, Fw 190F
II./SchG1	*Hauptman* F. Neubert	Fw 190A, Hs 123A
4,8./SchG1, 4./SchG2, Pz.St./JG51	*Hauptman* B. Meyer	Hs 129B
KG3	*Oberstleutnant* W. Lehwess-Litzmann	Ju 88A
I./KG3	*Hauptman* J. Jödicke	Ju 88A, Ju 88C
II./KG3	*Major* J. de Lalande	Ju 88A, Ju 88C
KG55	*Oberstleutnant* E. Kühl	He 111H
II./KG55	*Major* H. Höfer	He 111H
III./KG55	*Major* W. Antrup	He 111H
I./KG100	*Hauptman* H.G. Bätcher	He 111H
KG27	*Oberstleutnant* H.H. Beust	He 111H
I./KG27	*Hauptman* J. Petzold	He 111H
II./KG27	*Major* K.A. Petersen	He 111H
III./KG27	*Hauptman* K. Mayer	He 111H
JG52	*Oberstleutnant* D. Hrabak	Bf 109G
I./JG52	*Hauptman* H. Bennemann	Bf 109G
III./JG52	*Major* H. von Bonin	Bf 109G
II./JG3	*Hauptman* K. Brändle	Bf 109G
III./JG3	*Major* W. Ewald	Bf 109G

★ Combat strength of the Soviet 15th Air Army – north Kursk area – middle July 1943

Unit	Commander	Aircraft type
1st Guards Fighter Air Corps	Major General E.M. Beletskiy	
3rd GvIAD	Colonel V.P. Ukhov	La-5
4th GvIAD	Colonel V.A. Kitaev	Yak-1, Yak-7, Yak-9
234th IAD	Colonel E.Z. Tatanashvili	Yak-1, Yak-7, Yak-9
3nd Attack Air Corps	Major General M.I. Gorlachenko	
307th ShAD	Colonel A.V. Kozhemyakin	Il-2
308th ShAD	Colonel G.P. Turykin	Il-2
315th IAD	Colonel V.Ya. Litvinov	La-5
225th ShAD	Colonel A.F. Obukhov	Il-2
113rd BAD	Lieutenant General F.G. Michugin	Il-4
284th NBAD	Major G.P. Pokoevoy *	U-2
313rd NBAD	Colonel A.A. Voevodin	U-2
99th GvODRAP	Lieutenant Colonel N.P. Shchennikov	Pe-2

* from 23 July – Lieutenant Colonel I.A. Trushkin

★ Combat strength of the Soviet 1st Air Army – north Kursk area – middle July 1943

Unit	Commander	Aircraft type
2nd Fighter Air Corps	Lieutenant General A.S. Blagoveshchenskiy	
7th GvIAD	Major General V.M. Zabaluev	La-5
322nd IAD	Lieutenant Colonel M.P. Noga	Yak-1, Yak-7, Yak-9
8nd Fighter Air Corps	Major General F.F. Zherebchenko	
215th IAD	Colonel M.N. Yakushin	La-5
323rd IAD	Colonel P.P. Rybakov	Yak-1, Yak-7, Yak-9
2nd Bomber Air Corps	Major General V.A. Ushakov	
223rd BAD	Colonel F.P. Kotlyar	Pe-2
285th BAD	Colonel V.A. Sandalov	Pe-2
2nd Attack Air Corps	Major General V.V. Stepichev	
231st ShAD	Colonel L.A. Chizhikov	Il-2
232nd ShAD	Colonel A.G. Valkov	Il-2
303rd IAD	Major General G.N. Zakharov	Yak-1, Yak-7, Yak-9, La-5
309th IAD	Lieutenant Colonel V.N. Vuss	Yak-7, Yak-9, La-5
204th BAD	Colonel S.P. Andreev	Pe-2
224th ShAD	Colonel M.V. Kotelnikov	Il-2
233rd ShAD	Colonel V.V. Smirnov *	Il-2
311st ShAD	Colonel A.P. Troyan **	Il-2
213rd NBAD	Major General V.S. Molokov	U-2
102nd ODRAP	Lieutenant Colonel A.K. Rodin	Pe-2

* after the death of Colonel V.V. Smirnov on 27 July, the division was commanded by Lieutenant Colonel V.I. Smolovik
** from 30 July – Colonel V.V. Vasilyev

★ Combat strength of the Soviet 16th Air Army – north Kursk area – middle July 1943

Unit	Commander	Aircraft type
6nd Fighter Air Corps	Major General A.B. Yumashev	
273rd IAD	Colonel I.E. Fedorov	Yak-1, Yak-7, Yak-9
279th IAD	Colonel F.N. Dementiev	La-5
6nd Mixed Air Corps	Major General I.D. Antoshkin	
221st BAD	Colonel S.F. Buzylev	A-20B, Boston III
282nd IAD	Colonel A.M. Ryazanov *	Yak-1
3nd Bomber Air Corps	Major General A.Z. Karavatsky	
241st BAD	Colonel I.G. Kurylenko	Pe-2
301st BAD	Colonel F.M. Fedorenko	Pe-2
1st GvIAD	Lieutenant Colonel I.V. Krupenin	Yak-1, P-39
283rd IAD	Colonel S.P. Denisov	Yak-1, Yak-7
286th IAD	Colonel I.I. Ivanov	Yak-1, La-5
2nd GvShAD	Colonel G.I. Komarov	Il-2
299th ShAD	Colonel I.V. Krupskiy	Il-2
271st NBAD	Lieutenant Colonel K.P. Rasskazov **	U-2
16th ODRAP	D.S. Sherstyuk	A-20B, Pe-2
98th GvODRAP	Lieutenant Colonel B.P. Artemyev	Pe-2

* from 17 July – Lieutenant Colonel Yu.M. Berkal
** from 19 July – Colonel Kh.M. Borisenko

✠ Combat strength of the Luftwaffe 1st Air Division – north Kursk area – middle July 1943

Unit	Commander	Aircraft type
NAGr4	*Major* Toni Vinek	Bf 109G, Bf 110
NAGr10	*Oberleutnant* Werner Stein	Hs 126B, Fw 189A
NAGr15	*Major* Hubert Correns	Fw 189A
StG1	*Oberstleutnant* Gustav Pressler	Ju 87D
I./StG1	*Major* Horst Kaubisch	Ju 87D
II./StG1	*Hauptman* Ernst Otto	Ju 87D
III./StG1	*Hauptman* Friedrich Lang	Ju 87D
StG2	*Oberleutnant* Dr. Ernst Kupfer	Ju 87D
I./StG2	*Hauptman* Bruno Dilley	Ju 87D
III./StG2	*Hauptman* Walter Krauss	Ju 87D
III./StG3	*Major* Bernhard Hamester	Ju 87D
SchG1	*Major* Alfred Druschel	Bf 110G
I./SchG1	*Hauptman* Georg Dörffel	Fw 190A, Fw 190F
4,8./SchG1, 4./SchG2, Pz.St../JG51	*Führer der Panzerjägerstaffeln* (Fü.Pz.) *Hauptman* Bruno Meyer	Hs 129B
ZG1	*Oberstleutnant* Joachim Blechschmidt	Bf 110G
I./ZG1	*Hauptman* Wilfried Hermann	Bf 110E, Bf 110F, Bf 110G
KG51	*Major* Hanns Heise	Ju 88A
II./KG51	*Major* Herbert Voss	Ju 88A
III./KG51	*Hauptman* Wilhelm Rath	Ju 88A, Ju 88C
III./KG1	*Hauptman* Werner Kanther	Ju 88A, Ju 88C
KG4	*Oberstleutnant* Werner Klosinski	He 111H
II./KG4	*Major* Reinhard Graubner	He 111H
III./KG4	*Major* Kurt Neumann	He 111H
KG53	*Oberstleutnant* Fritz Pockrandt	He 111H
II./KG53	*Major* Herbert Wittmann	He 111H
III./KG53	*Major* Emil Allmendinger	He 111H
JG51	*Oberstleutnant* Karl-Gottfried Nordmann	Fw 190A
I./JG51	*Major* Erich Leie	Fw 190A
III./JG51	*Hauptman* Fritz Losigkeit	Fw 190A
IV./JG51	*Major* Hans Ekkehard Bob	Fw 190A
III./JG52	*Hauptman* Günther Rall	Bf 109G
I./JG54	*Major* Gerhard Homuth	Fw 190A
II./JG54	*Hauptman* Heinrich Jung	Fw 190A

Note: Along with the indicated units, the groups and units which were under direct subordination to the 6th Air Fleet Headquarters, participated in the battle: IV./NJG5, FAGr2, St., I, II./TG3, St., II./TG4, Verb. (S) 5, as well as communication, liaison, ambulance, and night attack units.

★ Combat strength of the Soviet 5th Air Army – south Kursk area – beginning of August 1943

Unit	Commander	Aircraft type
4th Fighter Air Corps	Major General I.D. Podgorny	
294th IAD	Colonel I.A. Taranenko	Yak-1, Yak-7
302nd IAD	Colonel B.I. Litvinov	La-5
1st Bomber Air Corps	Colonel I.S. Polbin	
1st GvBAD	Colonel F.I. Dobysh	Pe-2
293rd BAD	Colonel G.V. Gribakin	Pe-2
1st Attack Air Corps	Lieutenant General V.G. Ryazanov	
266th ShAD	Colonel F.G. Rodyakin	Il-2
292nd ShAD	Major General F.A. Agaltsov	Il-2
203rd IAD	Major General K.G. Baranchuk	Yak-1
511th ORAP	Major A.A. Babanov	Pe-2

★ Combat strength of the Soviet 2nd Air Army – south Kursk area – beginning August 1943

Unit	Commander	Aircraft type
5th Fighter Air Corps	Major General D.P. Galunov	
256th IAD	Lieutenant Colonel N.S. Gerasimov	Yak-7, Yak-9
8th GvIAD	Colonel I.P. Laryushkin	La-5
10th Fighter Air Corps	Major General M.M. Golovnya	
201st IAD	Lieutenant Colonel F.V. Vladimirov *	Yak-1, Yak-7, La-5
235th IAD	Major General I.A. Lakeev	La-5
5th Attack Air Corps	Lieutenant General N.P. Kamanin	
4th GvShAD	Major General G.F. Baydukov	Il-2
264th ShAD	Colonel N.I. Olenev	Il-2
202nd BAD	Colonel S.I. Nechiporenko	Pe-2
291st ShAD	Major General A.N. Vitruk	Il-2
208th NBAD	Colonel L.N. Yuzeev	U-2, R-5
454th BAP	Major A.A. Tatulov	A-20B
50th Reconn. Air Regiment	Lieutenant Colonel I.Ya. Mironov	Pe-2

* from 16 August – Colonel V.A. Sryvkin
Note: In the course of the defence battle, the 205th IAD was withdrawn to the rear, while the 256th IAD (commander – Colonel N.S. Gerasimov) was introduced into the strength of the 5th Fighter Air Corps.

✚ Combat strength of the Luftwaffe 8th Air Corps – south Kursk area – beginning August 1943

Unit	Commander	Aircraft type
NAGr6	*Hauptmann* Heribert Rinke	Bf 109G, Bf 110G, Hs 126B, Fw 189A
2(F)./11		Ju 88D
StG2	*Major* Dr. Ernst Kupfer	Ju 87D
I./StG2	*Hauptmann* Bruno Dilley	Ju 87D
II./StG2	*Hauptmann* Hans-Karl Stepp	Ju 87D, Ju 87G
III./StG2	*Hauptmann* Hans-Ulrich Rudel	Ju 87D
StG77	*Major* Helmut Bruck	Ju 87D
I./StG77	*Major* Werner Roell	Ju 87D
II./StG77	*Hauptmann* Helmut Leicht	Ju 87D
III./StG77	*Hauptmann* Franz Kieslich	Ju 87D
II./SchG1	*Hauptmann* Frank Neubert	Fw 190A, Fw 190F, Hs 123A
4,8./SchG1, 4,8./SchG2	*Führer der Panzerjägerstaffeln* (Fü.Pz.) *Hauptmann* Bruno Meyer	Hs 129B
KG3	*Oberstleutnant* Walter Lehwess-Litzmann	Ju 88A
I./KG3	*Major* Joachim Jödicke	Ju 88A, Ju 88C
KG55	*Oberstleutnant* Dr. Ernst Kühl	He 111H
II./KG55	*Major* Heinz Höfer	He 111H
III./KG55	*Major* Wilhelm Antrup	He 111H
I./KG100	*Major* Hans-Georg Bätcher	He 111H
KG27	*Oberstleutnant* Freiherr von Beust	He 111H
I./KG27	*Hauptmann* Joachim Petzold	He 111H
III./KG27	*Hauptmann* Karl Mayer	He 111H
JG52	*Oberstleutnant* Dietrich Hrabak	Bf 109G
I./JG52	*Hauptmann* Johannes Wiese	Bf 109G
II./JG52	*Hauptmann* Gerhard Barkhorn	Bf 109G
III./JG52	*Hauptmann* Günther Rall	Bf 109G

Note: Along with the indicated units, the groups and units which were under direct subordination to the 4th Air Fleet Headquarters, participated in the battle: FAGr4, Verb. (S) 4, as well as communication. liaison, ambulance, and night attack units.

◑ Shot-down Yak-1 fighter.

Appendix II – Combat Sorties

★ Number of Soviet combat sorties – north Kursk area – 5th to 11th July 1943

Date	16th Air Army		Long-Range Aviation	6th Air Fleet	
	Day	Night		Day	Night
5 July	1,147	85	17	2,088	0
6 July	1,126	200	269	1,023	15
7 July	1,185	212	210	1,687	92
8 July	913	173	169	1,173	134
9 July	956	145	36	877	0
10 July	671	173	77	1,136	3
11 July	301	176	0	933	51
Total	6,299	1,164	778	8,917	295

★ Number of Soviet combat sorties – south Kursk area – 5th to 18th July 1943

Date	2nd Air Army		17th Air Army		Long Range Aviation*	4th Air Fleet	
	Day	Night	Day	Night		Day	Night
5 July	1,322	48	446	123	0	2,387	0
6 July	820	72	458	197	85	1,686	26
7 July	847	83	689	192	163	1,829	64
8 July	957	96	228	174	275	1,686	57
9 July	658	60	187	183	161	1,621	28
10 July	455	69	71	149	231	682	17
11 July	539	57	56	183	45	1,039	18
12 July	759	109	134	164	0	654	61
13 July	659	156	118	151	112	656	0
14 July	865	200	168	114	144	1,452	28
15 July	328	151	35	146	193	706	40
16 July	723	219	203	143	112	499	111
17 July	484	135	0	0	0	138	85
18 July	436	199	0	0	0	79	27
Total	9,804	2,793	2,793	1,919	1,521	15,114	562

* long-range aviation sorties performed on the Voronezh and Central Fronts are taken into account.

★ Soviet bomb type usage (%) in north Kursk salient 12th July till 18th August 1943

Unit	HE bombs	Fragmentation bombs	Anti-tank bombs	Incendiary bombs	Flare bombs
1st Air Army *	62.6	31.4	4.6	0.8	0.6
15th Air Army	41.3	55.0	2.4	0.9	0.4
16th Air Army	64.2	31.5	2.5	1.0	0.8
ADD	80.0	–	–	15.0	5.0

* combat sorties from 12 until 28 July only

★ ✚ Day & night combat sorties – north Kursk area – 12th July to 18th August 1943

Date	1st Air Army	15th Air Army	16th Air Army	Total Red Army Air Force Total Luftwaffe	6th Air Fleet
12 July	868	1,037	269	2,174	1,126
13 July	942	946	250	2,138	1,133
14 July	945	598	164	1,707	914
15 July	618	792	1,002	2,442	982
16 July	737	766	1,713	3,216	2,065
17 July	948	1,043	1,743	3,734	1,993
18 July	632	649	544	1,825	1,435
19 July	490	1,273	1,222	2,985	1,746
20 July	469	657	1,122	2,248	1,232
21 July	660	762	497	1,919	1,525
22 July	521	773	1,105	2,339	1,408
23 July	333	476	276	1,085	1,164
24 July	202	610	376	1,188	1,623
25 July	134	785	821	1,740	519
26 July	361	290	49	700	525
27 July	395	15	200	610	907
28 July	575	111	600	1,286	992
29 July	–	150	326	476	522
30 July	–	276	321	597	547
31 July	–	662	294	956	1,692
1 August	–	969	808	1,777	1,897
2 August	–	786	1,312	2,098	1,655
3 August	–	1,055	949	2,004	1,437
4 August	–	1,196	1,018	2,214	1,451
5 August	–	787	1,022	1,809	1,429
6 August	–	877	420	1,297	839
7 August	–	987	466	1,453	1,451
8 August	–	599	600	1,199	1,051
9 August	–	490	366	856	825
10 August	–	487	258	745	621
11 August	–	247	323	570	613
12 August	–	994	405	1,399	1,038
13 August	–	538	210	748	806
14 August	–	734	165	899	1,052
15 August	–	337	424	761	446
16 August	–	129	344	473	470
17 August	–	243	406	649	495
18 August	–	28	46	74	609
Total	9,860	24,154	22,436	56,450	42,235

* long-range aviation not taken into account

★ ✚ Day & night combat sorties – south Kursk area – 3rd to 20th August 1943

Date	2nd Air Army		5th Air Army Day	Total Red Army AF	8th Air Corps		Total Luftwaffe
	Day	Night			Day	Night	
3 August	1,264	292	1,115	2,671	521	13	534
4 August	736	256	916	1,908	1,119	14	1,133
10 August	604	75	507	1,186	1,033	17	1,050
11 August	380	38	236	654	1,108	6	1,114
12 August	580	145	406	1,131	1,209	13	1,222
13 August	359	94	452	905	975	15	990
14 August	542	123	516	1,181	1,103	22	1,125
15 August	270	263	659	1,192	1,177	19	1,196
16 August	214	163	228	605	818	10	828
17 August	590	178	269	1,037	600	4	604
18 August	476	54	797	1,327	785	8	793
19 August	519	289	524	1,332	758	9	767
20 August	379	287	502	1,168	1,018	11	1,029
Total	6,913	2,257	7,127	16,297	12,224	12,224	161

* Soviet long-range aviation and German light and night-fighter aviation not taken into account
Note: No German data for the other dates of August have been found. According to Soviet sources, from 3 until 23 August the 2nd Air Army carried out 14,648 combat sorties, the 5th Air Army – 12,172 sorties.

★ Soviet combat sorties – north Kursk area – 12th July till 18th August 1943

Unit	Combat sorties					Total	Average no of sorties per day
	Fighters	Attack aircraft	Day bombers	Night bombers	Recon aircraft		
1st Air Army *	3,923	2,042	120	3,068	707	9,860	580
15th Air Army	8,517	4,397	463	9,465	1,312	24,154	636
16th Air Army	6,284	3,794	3,507	7,429	1,422	22,436	641
ADD	–	–	–	4,545	–	4,545	120
Total	18,724	10,233	4,090	24,507	3,441	60,995	1,977

* combat sorties from 12 until 28 July only

★ Soviet combat sorties – north Kursk area – 12th July till 18th August 1943

Main Tasks	Combat sorties				Total	%
	1st Air Army *	15th Air Army	16th Air Army	ADD		
Strikes on troops and equipment	5,166	11,969	14,595	2,162	33,892	56
Strikes on railway traffic	72	2,210	238	1,887	4,407	7
Strikes on airfields	48	146	61	496	751	1
Air cover of ground troops	1,750	4,567	1,826	–	8,143	13
Air cover for attack aircraft and bombers	2,117	3,950	4,294	–	10,361	17
Reconnaissance	707	1,312	1,422	–	3,441	6
Total	9,860	24,154	22,436	4,545	60,995	100

* combat sorties from 12 until 28 July only

Appendix III – Arrivals & Losses

✠ Aircraft arrivals and losses of Luftwaffe 8th Air Corps – July 1943

Unit	Aircraft Type	Quantity as of 30/06/43	Arrivals				Losses					Quantity as of 31/07/43
			New	After Repairs	From other units	Total	Combat losses	Non-combat losses	Sent for repair	Sent to other units	Total	
II./JG3	Bf 109G	33	39	2	1	42	24	9	0	6	39	36
III./JG3	Bf 109G	40	23	5	5	33	20	9	3	0	32	41
Stab./JG52	Bf 109G	4	3	0	0	3	1	2	0	1	4	3
I./JG52	Bf 109G	34	25	0	1	26	21	8	0	0	29	31
III./JG52	Bf 109G	42	9	0	4	13	13	7	6	0	26	29
Stab./StG2	Ju 87D	3	1	0	0	1	0	0	1	1	2	2
I./StG2	Ju 87D	37	7	2	15	24	8	6	5	6	25	36
II./StG2	Ju 87D	36	11	3	3	17	9	6	5	3	23	30
	Ju 87G	0	1	0	8	9	0	0	0	0	0	9
III./StG2	Ju 87D	35	11	0	13	24	18	2	3	3	26	33
Stab./StG77	Ju 87D	3	3	0	0	3	0	0	2	1	3	3
I./StG77	Ju 87D	40	14	3	0	17	6	9	1	0	16	41
II./StG77	Ju 87D	41	21	2	1	24	4	1	21	0	26	39
III./StG77	Ju 87D	36	12	6	3	21	10	0	9	0	19	38
Stab./KG27	He 111H	2	0	0	0	0	0	0	0	0	0	2
I./KG27	He 111H	21	0	7	0	7	11	4	1	0	16	12
II./KG27	He 111H	34	13	0	3	16	9	4	2	1	16	34
III./KG27	He 111H	34	11	3	5	19	17	1	2	3	23	30
14./KG27	He 111H	10	0	2	0	2	1	1	0	0	2	10
Stab./KG55	He 111H	4	1	0	0	1	0	1	0	0	1	4
II./KG55	He 111H	47	10	2	3	15	9	1	4	15	29	33
III./KG55	He 111H	46	5	3	0	8	4	3	0	2	9	45
I./KG100	He 111H	38	3	0	0	3	8	3	5	0	16	25
Stab./KG3	Ju 88A	1	2	0	0	2	1	0	0	1	2	1
I./KG3	Ju 88A/C	34	25	2	0	27	7	2	11	1	21	40
II./KG3	Ju 88A/C	37	18	11	1	30	12	8	7	0	27	40
Stab./SchG1	Fw 190A/F	0	4	0	0	4	0	0	0	0	0	4
I./SchG1	Fw 190A	52	19	0	0	19	16	14	8	5	43	28
II./SchG1	Fw 190A/F	33	25	1	0	26	13	14	0	6	33	26
	Hs 123B	16	0	2	0	2	4	2	1	0	7	11
4./SchG1	Hs 129B	17	2	0	3	5	8	2	0	4	14	8
8./SchG1	Hs 129B	16	3	0	0	3	11	3	0	0	14	5
4./SchG2	Hs 129B	17	7	0	1	8	6	4	0	3	13	12
8./SchG2	Hs 129B	10	6	0	2	8	0	1	0	1	2	16
Pz.St./JG51	Hs 129B	15	6	1	3	10	10	3	1	0	14	11
2(F)./11	Ju 88D	10	6	0	0	6	3	3	1	0	7	9
1(H)./21	Fw 189A	10	1	0	0	1	0	0	2	0	2	9
2(H)./33	Bf 110G	8	1	0	0	1	2	0	0	0	2	7
1./NAGr2	Bf 109G	13	7	0	1	8	1	1	1	2	5	16
2(H)./16	Fw 189A	10	3	0	0	3	3	0	0	0	3	10
5(H)./32	Hs 126B	9	4	0	10	14	2	0	6	0	8	15
Total		928	362	57	86	505	292	134	108	65	599	834

Note: A: By the end of July 1943, most of the above groups and units were withdrawn from the 8th Air Corps.
    B: About two thirds of German losses were related to support given to the 'Group South' armies during the Kursk offensive.

★ Aircraft arrivals and losses of Soviet 2nd Air Army – July 1943

Unit	As of 01 July 1943	Arrived				Losses					As of 31 July 1943
		New arrivals	From other units	After repair	Total	Transfer to other units	Sent for repair	Combat losses	Non-combat losses	Total	
1st BAK	117	12	0	0	12	0	0	36	6	42	87
1st ShAK *	206/82	20/12	0/0	0/0	20/12	0/0	2/1	71/28	4/2	77/31	149/63
5th IAK	278	1	46	1	48	66	2	117	9	194	132
4th IAK	184	23	0	0	23	0	1	61	3	65	142
291th ShAD *	100/28	71/27	18/0	2/0	91/27	0/0	57/12	91/19	6/1	154/32	37/23
208th NBAD	57	0	86	5	91	33	0	3	4	40	108
454th BAP	21	6	2	0	8	6	0	4	0	10	19
Total	1073	172	152	8	332	105	75	430	35	645	760

* denotes the number of attack / fighter aircraft
Note: Some of the figures do not correspond to other sources. Thus, as of 01/08/43, the 4th IAK had 131 fighters, while the 291st ShAD had 93 attack aircraft and 35 fighters, and possibly these changes were introduced on the last day of the month. Also note the 5th ShAK and 10th IAK, which became a part of 2nd Air Army in the end of July, are not counted.

★ Aircrew losses of the Soviet 16th Air Army – July 1943

Unit	Regiment Commanders	Regiment Navigators	Squadron Commanders and Deputies	Flight Commanders	Pilots	Flight Observers	Gunners/ Radio Ops	Air Gunners	Total
3rd BAK	0	0	3	0	25	31	28	0	87
221st BAD	0	0	4	1	9	15	17	20	66
271st NBAD	0	0	1	0	6	6	0	0	13
Total – Bomber	**0**	**0**	**8**	**1**	**40**	**52**	**45**	**20**	**166**
2nd GvShAD	0	1	4	0	38	0	0	39	82
299th ShAD	0	0	7	10	62	0	0	65	144
Total – Attack	**0**	**1**	**11**	**10**	**100**	**0**	**0**	**104**	**226**
6th IAK	2	0	10	2	46	0	0	0	60
1st GvIAD	0	1	13	0	21	0	0	0	35
283th IAD	0	0	1	2	13	0	0	0	16
286th IAD	0	0	9	2	50	0	0	0	61
282nd IAD	0	0	3	2	7	0	0	0	12
Total – Fighter	**2**	**1**	**36**	**8**	**137**	**0**	**0**	**0**	**184**
16th, 98th ODRAP	0	0	0	1	2	3	3	1	10
Total	**2**	**2**	**55**	**20**	**279**	**55**	**48**	**125**	**586**

★ Aircraft arrivals and losses of Soviet 2nd Air Army – August 1943

Unit	As of 01 August 1943	Arrived				Losses					As of 31 August 1943
		New arrivals	From other units	After repair	Total	Transfer to other units	Sent for repair	Combat losses	Non-combat losses	Total	
5th IAK	132	99	41	1	141	1	62	62	6	131	142
10th IAK	196	0	82	0	82	0	38	97	13	148	130
5th ShAK	132	74	4	0	78	0	19	78	3	100	110
202nd BAD	92	30	0	0	30	0	2	18	1	21	101
291st ShAD*	93/35	22/20	9/1	1/0	32/21	0/0	33/22	22/12	8/7	63/41	62/15
208th NBAD	108	0	1	2	3	0	14	5	1	20	91
454th BAP	19	4	2	1	7	0	0	7	1	8	18
Total	807	249	140	5	394	1	190	301	40	532	669

*attack aircraft/fighters.
Note: Some sources give different data. For example, as of 01 September 1943 the 10th IAK had 172 fighters, the 5th ShAK – 12 aircraft, and the 291st ShAD – 72 attack aircraft and 26 fighters. Possibly, the changes were introduced on the last day of the month.

★ Aircraft losses of the Soviet 16th Air Army – July 1943

Unit	Combat Losses							Non-Combat Losses			Total	No of sorties per combat loss	No of sorties per non-combat loss
	Shot down by enemy	Not returned	Shot down by artillery	Forced landing	Other	Ground loss at airfield	Total	Crashes	Accident	Total			
3rd BAK	10	14	0	7	6	9	46	0	2	2	48	41	795
221st BAD	19	16	0	1	0	0	36	2	0	2	38	36	40
271st NBAD	0	2	0	3	1	2	8	1	4	5	13	727	125
Total - Bomber	**29**	**32**	**0**	**11**	**7**	**11**	**90**	**3**	**6**	**9**	**99**	**91**	**255**
2nd GvShAD	17	14	2	12	9	3	57	1	6	7	64	31	16
299th ShAD	23	22	0	46	0	0	91	2	4	6	97	19	35
Total - Attack	**40**	**36**	**2**	**58**	**9**	**3**	**148**	**3**	**10**	**13**	**161**	**24**	**26**
6th IAK	60	6	0	28	0	3	97	0	0	0	97	23	0
1st GvIAD	52	1	0	0	0	0	53	1	0	1	54	23	290
283th IAD	15	3	0	6	0	0	24	0	2	2	26	69	105
286th IAD	11	4	0	42	10	0	67	0	4	4	71	24	86
282nd IAD	13	0	0	8	0	0	21	0	0	0	21	59	0
Total - Fighter	**151**	**14**	**0**	**84**	**10**	**3**	**262**	**1**	**6**	**7**	**269**	**31**	**195**
16th, 98th ODRAP	4	0	0	1	0	0	5	0	1	1	6	43	0
Total	**224**	**82**	**2**	**154**	**26**	**17**	**505**	**7**	**23**	**30**	**535**	**39**	**133**

✠ Aircraft arrivals and losses of Luftwaffe fighter units – August 1943

Unit	As of 01 August 1943	Arrived				Losses					As of 31 August 1943
		Reinforcements	From other units	From repair	Total	Transfer to other units	To repair	Combat losses	Non-combat losses	Total	
St../JG51	23 Fw 190A	4	5	0	9	10	0	4	3	17	15
	2 Bf 109G	0	0	0	0	0	0	0	1	1	1
I./JG51	36 Fw 190A	21	3	5	29	0	3	12	15	30	35
III./JG51	36 Fw 190A	8	11	5	24	3	4	13	12	32	28
IV./JG51	35 Bf 109G	31	0	0	31	4	0	16	14	34	32
15./JG51	17 Fw 190A	0	12	3	15	0	0	8	5	13	19
I./JG54	35 Fw 190A	14	2	0	16	0	0	11	17	28	23
II./JG54	7 Bf 109G	0	0	0	0	5	0	0	2	7	0
	26 Fw 190A	3	21	0	24	1	3	12	12	28	22
St../JG52	3 Bf 109G	1	0	0	1	2	0	0	0	2	2
I./JG52	31 Bf 109G	25	21	4	50	4	18	11	13	46	35
II./JG52	32 Bf 109G	8	5	14	27	14	2	3	3	22	37
III./JG52	29 Bf 109G	34	6	0	40	0	4	22	12	38	31
Total	**312**	**149**	**86**	**31**	**266**	**43**	**34**	**112**	**109**	**298**	**280**

Note: Groups II and III../JG3 are not included, as they were withdrawn to the West at the beginning of August.

Appendix IV – Knights Cross

Date	Rank	Pilot	Unit	Aircraft Type	Serial Number	Tactical Number	Area Where Lost	Note
5 July	*Hauptmann*	H. Michael	III./KG1	Ju 88A-14	144659	V4+AS	To the east of Podolyan	Awarded Posthumously
7 July	*Hauptmann*	K.A. Pape	III./StG1 (3./StG1 ¿¿)	Ju 87D-3	110041	L1+AL	Krasavka, 20km west of Ponyri	
8 July	*Oberfeldwebel*	H. Strassl	III./JG51	Fw 190A-4	142351	«Черная 4»	To the south of Ponyri	Awarded Posthumously
8 July	*Hauptmann*	B. Wutka	III./StG2	Ju 87D-3	110045	VT+ZO	To the east of Verkhopenye	
8 July	*Oberleutnant*	K. Fitzner	II./StG77	Ju 87D-3	131075		Syrtsovo	
9 July	*Oberfeldwebel*	E. Rossmann	III./JG52	Bf 109G-6	20154	«Белая 4»	To the south of Bely Kolodez	Captured by the 'Krasnaya Volna' workers collective farm
11 July	*Major*	R. Resch	IV./JG51	Fw 190A-5	157264		To the north of Yudinka, 4km to the south-west of Maloarkhangelsk	
14 July	*Major*	W. Ewald	III./JG3	Bf 109G-6	20220	« + I	In the vicinity of Shakhovo	Opened parachute at altitude of 50m over the top of the Soviet 375th Rifle Division. Captured.
14 July	*Oberleutnant*	G. Schmidt	II./StG2	Ju 87D-3	100345	T6+EN	Vinogradovks, 1km to the north-east of Belenikhino	

Note: Some sources indicate that *Hauptmann*. A. Kuntze was supposedly Killed In Action over Kursk, however, as Commander of IV./KG26, he was also listed as Missing In Action July 5 1943 over the North Sea – far away from the Soviet-German front.

↻ One of the pilots of I./ZG1 after a combat sortie. At the end of July the group was withdrawn from the Eastern Front. The unit had lost twelve Messerschmitts since 5 July, and the same number of aircraft were transported to Germany for repairs.

Index

¶ references a picture
§ references a colour profile
¤ references a table